STERLING IN

Sir Alan Walters is Professor of
Economics at Johns Hopkins University,
Maryland, and was Personal Economic Adviser to the Prime Minister, 1981-84 and 1989.
He has written extensively in the fields of
transport economics, econometrics, monetary
economics and macro-economic policy; his
most recent publication was *Britain's Economic
Renaissance* (1986).

Sterling in Danger

The Economic Consequences of Pegged Exchange Rates

ALAN WALTERS

FONTANA/Collins

Published in association with the Institute of Economic Affairs

The Institute of Economic Affairs was set up as a research and educational trust under a trust deed signed in 1955. It began regular publication in 1957 with specialised studies of markets and prices. It is a company limited by guarantee, controlled by Managing Trustees, and independent of any political party.

First published in 1990 by Fontana Paperbacks
8 Grafton Street, London W1X 3LA

Copyright © Sir Alan Walters 1990

ISBN 0-00-637673-8

Printed and bound in Great Britain by
Collins, Glasgow

Conditions of Sale

This book is sold subject to the condition that it shall not, by way of trade or otherwise, be lent, re-sold, hired out or otherwise circulated without the publisher's prior consent in any form of binding or cover other than that in which it is published and without a similar condition including this condition being imposed on the subsequent purchaser.

CONTENTS

He is convinced that monetary
policy = manipulating money
supply. Several places where
'interest rates' move by market
forces — e.g. demand for loans P 31

Spain '85

Main worry : don't know which
   rate is 'right'

PREFACE

THIS BOOK attempts to throw some light on a long-standing debate on exchange rate policy. Should the authorities determine monetary policy and allow the exchange rate to float where it will, or should the exchange rate be fixed and monetary policy follow whatever path is needed to validate that parity? To fix or not to fix, however, is not the only question. We have been urged to avoid such 'extreme' solutions, to get the best of both worlds, to have our cake and eat it. In short, to adopt 'fixed but flexible systems', 'crawling pegs', 'reference zones', and above all to join the Exchange Rate Mechanism of the European Monetary System. In the aftermath of the Single European Act (1985) and the Delors Report of 1989, the Commission of the European Community has promoted the cause of a monetary union of Europe (EMU) to the top of the agenda. One Europe, one money.

The consequences of an exchange rate régime, monetary policies and currency union are wide ranging, profound and subject to great uncertainty. My purpose is to provide a basic understanding of exchange rates and associated monetary policy. History is replete with sad stories of the distress and inflations caused by politicians imposing their own ideas of appropriate rates of exchange. In Chapter 1 I allude to the great 1925 error of Britain returning to the old gold standard and the deflations and slump that ensued. We need to be reminded of the lessons of the past. But the main focus of this book is more recent events — namely, the record of the ERM/EMS, Britain's flirtation with the ERM in 1987/88, and the likely economic consequences of entry in the 1990s.

One cannot write on policy without occasionally discussing political, psychological and social aspects. My purpose, however, is largely limited to examining the *economics of policy*. I am not qualified to pass judgement on the socio-political aspects of policy. And many observers would consider the socio-political aspects of the emergence of a new union of Europe the more important part of the story. Perhaps so. But I stick to my last.

It was at the insistence of Professor Deepak Lal and Graham Mather that I embarked on this book. Subsequently, many read the manuscript and saved me from serious error. I am most grateful to Tim Congdon, Walter Eltis, Anthony de Jasay, Patrick Minford, Gordon Pepper, Arthur Seldon and Geoffrey Wood. I believe that I took on board all their amendments and suggestions — but, of course, the usual exonerations are due. For preparing the manuscript for publication I am grateful to Walter Allan, Ruth Croxford and Michael Solly — all gave that IEA support which makes publishing an author's pleasure.

Washington DC
May 1990   ALAN WALTERS

FLOATING AND ANCHORING CURRENCIES

Fise & Float & dirty fise

Two Fixes — 1924 and 1987

IN THE LONG record of financial history, monies have normally been either commodities, such as silver or gold, or titles to specific quantities of such metals. In fact, since 1717 Britain has spent more than 200 years with a gold convertible currency. During wars and their aftermath, gold convertibility was usually suspended but was resumed again after a period of inconvertible paper currency.

Under the exigencies of the First World War, Britain decreed the gold-inconvertibility of the pound and allowed sterling to float. The post-war inflation and rapid deflation, as well as the 1923 hyperinflation in Germany, gave graphic evidence of the fragility of irredeemable paper currencies. An anchor was required. In the mid-1920s, therefore, it seemed entirely natural to return to the standard which had served the Western countries well in the previous half-century — gold. After eight years of a floating exchange rate, in 1925 Churchill, then Chancellor of the Exchequer, chose to peg the pound at the equivalent of the pre-war parity of $4.86 (the United States dollar was convertible into gold at $34 per fine ounce).

In one of the great economic tracts of the 20th century, *The Economic Consequences of Mr Churchill* (1925), John Maynard Keynes argued that the return to the pre-war gold parity for sterling would entail the most painful deflation of British prices and wages. Keynes said that at a stroke it would render uncompetitive much of industry, and particularly the great export trades such as coal. Keynes proved to be right. In particular, the pressure to reduce wages and make coal exports profitable led to the strikes of 1926, which embittered workers and exacerbated class conflicts for many years. True, Britain continued to grow in 1926-28, but at a low rate compared with the United States and Germany. Finally, the high value of sterling exacted its toll in full measure when the world economy suffered a sharp downturn in 1929. The dole queues lengthened dramatically and output fell sharply. Only when, in 1931, Britain went off the gold standard did the economy show signs of recovery. With a floating rate from 1931, Britain's recovery proceeded until overtaken by the rumblings of the Second World War.

The return to a golden anchor had validated all Keynes's dire predictions. He saw the advantages of an anchor, but he condemned the tight golden chain which would pull the ship underwater; he wanted enough chain to manoeuvre the ship of state. Keynes knew that the First World War had seen the end of the old gold standard. Countries were no longer prepared to follow the old golden rules: allowing the money supply to contract when they lost, and to expand when they gained, gold reserves. Governments wanted to have their cake and eat it. More than ever before the First World War, they wished to tailor their domestic monetary policy to their need to create jobs, rather than to allow the gold flows to dictate monetary contraction and further recession. This fundamental dilemma was put succinctly in 1923 by Keynes in yet another great tract.[1] If there is a conflict between the policy requirements for domestic conditions and the policy needed for international obligations, then, argued Keynes, domestic objectives should take precedence. Certainly in those years between the two world wars, Keynes was proved to be right.

The 1980s: Same Dilemma, More Choices
In the 1980s, alas, we faced the same dilemma but with no Keynes. The menu of choice, however, had been widened. In the 1920s Churchill's choice was between floating and joining the gold standard at a truly fixed rate. It was expected

that the parity would 'never' be adjusted (except under the then unthinkable conditions of another world war), and the rate was to be kept within the 'gold points' — about one-half of 1 per cent. By the 1980s, however, we had experienced the 'fixed but flexible', or pseudo-fixed, system of Bretton Woods and, in the 1970s and 1980s, the European 'snake' and its successor, the European Monetary System (EMS). These systems eventually became quite free from any gold anchor. They provided for much more variation about the par value (plus or minus 2.25 per cent and even 6 per cent in the case of the EMS). Furthermore, after consultation and some sort of agreement, the par or central value could be realigned. With a bureaucratic logic, these 'fixed but flexible' or 'pegged' systems were thought to capture the best of the truly fixed anchor and the best of the free, flexible float. The central banks could keep their power to create money at their (or their governments') discretion to control demand, while at the same time an anchor (albeit a rather dragging anchor), not to gold but to a trusted currency such as the Deutschemark in the 1980s, would prevent inflation or deflation getting out of hand. Thus the great nations of continental Europe (and Eire) flexibly fixed their currencies to the D-mark. But sterling, because of its special status as a widely used international currency and because of North Sea oil, did not join the Exchange Rate Mechanism (ERM) of the EMS.

During the 1980s there have been many campaigns to induce Britain to join the ERM. It has been widely represented as a touchstone of the degree of commitment to the European Community or to the objective of a monetary union of Europe. Much of the support for joining the EMS rests not so much on economic argument as on political conviction and concern about 'missing the Eurobus', two-tier Europe, and on a forlorn Britain excluded from the great blocs of the rest of the world. But as is so often the case, political persuasion and debate, in its search for allegiances and support, ignores critical differences in economic analysis and policy. One of the main themes of this book is that, in

11

economic terms, one can see much virtue in either absolutely free exchange rates or, alternatively, in a monetary union with a unified currency; yet the pseudo-fixed system of the ERM is an anathema and inherently flawed. Consequently, in *economic* terms, it is quite sensible to have serious reservations about the EMS/ERM but to be an enthusiast for some particular forms of monetary union.

The unity of Europe was also a major difference compared with Churchill's inter-war uncertainties. European union was far from Churchill's mind, whereas today Euro-union proceeds at a rattling pace. In 1925, Churchill looked towards what appeared to be the only safe anchorage the world had known — gold convertibility. Keynes might well rail against gold as a 'barbaric relic', but gold had always been the refuge of any responsible government after periods with an inconvertible paper currency. The dollar then was 'as good as gold' — with no fears about inconvertibility. And so the dollar was disciplined by the promise of the Federal Reserve Board (the Fed) to redeem dollars in gold.

By the 1980s, however, all states had long since cut themselves loose from the gold anchor. Nor had any other commodities, or bundles of commodities, replaced gold. (This had occurred formally when the United States severed the gold link, but in reality convertibility had been much diminished in the years after the Second World War.) When the British government decided to peg sterling in 1987, it was not to gold but to the Bundesbank's Deutschemark. And the Bundesbank had abolished gold convertibility almost two decades earlier.

The consequences of the fix of 1926 were severe. As Keynes so powerfully argued, the return to the gold standard at $4.86 rendered British exports (particularly of coal) uncompetitive on world markets, so the only possible adjustment for British prices and wages was for them to fall. And Keynes rightly predicted that the only way they could fall was by a prolonged recession. In 1926 Britain began the downswing into the Great Depression. Not until 1931, when sterling was floated free of its gold anchor and depreciated, did Britain begin to emerge from the slump. The cost of Mr Churchill was far greater than even Keynes had calculated. And the divisiveness and distortions of that period remain with us, in muted form, even to this day.

In 1987 sterling was pegged at 3.00 (or rather, strictly, just below 3) Deutschemarks. True, this was no official peg, but the markets were given to believe that 3.00 was the appropriate value and that the Treasury and the Bank would jolly well see that it stuck. Everyone believed it. Why 3.00 and not 3.30 or 2.70? It is not clear why this value was chosen as the pegging level — partly, one supposes, because it had been hovering near three at the time, or perhaps because it is a nice round number. If one wished to provide a rationalisation consistent with economic theory, one would have to argue that 3.00 was close to and, under expected differential inflation rates, was likely to remain close to the 'fundamental real equilibrium exchange rate' (FREER) — an elusive concept that will worry me, if not you the reader, in Chapter 2.

Consequences of the 1925 Fix 'Disastrous'

The 1925 fix was much more disastrous than that of 1987. Instead of the six years of absolute fixity to 1931, the wobbly peg of 1987 did not make it through a second year. In 1925 Churchill fixed *above* the market value, making sterling too dear, whereas in 1987 sterling was pegged initially *below* the market value, making the pound too cheap. Instead of the General Strike of 1926 and the depression and deflation of the 1930s, the pegging of sterling in 1987 launched Britain into a boom and inflation. Soon thereafter, the inflation and the rise in interest rates required to control the monetary growth and prevent that dreaded 'free-fall' of sterling ensured that a marked slowdown, even a recession, would be required in order to restore price stability.

The consequences of returning to gold in 1925 included a breakdown of the international trade and monetary systems, massive trade restrictions, ultimately exchange controls, and all the curious panoply of agricultural support and 'reconstruction' measures that are still with us in one form or another. The short peg of 1987, I believe, is likely to have no such long-term consequences. It is plausible to suppose that it will be but a 'blip' (but rather a large one) on the third Thatcher Government's record, and that open commodity and financial markets will continue to be the proud result of the Thatcher renaissance.

Fixes, Floats and Fudges in Exchange Rates

Underlying much of the discussion of international monetary arrangements in the 1970s and 1980s has been the yearning for some *system*. The present arrangements in which the major currencies — dollar, Deutschemark and yen — float more or less freely against one another, is often called, pejoratively, the *non-system*. Notwithstanding the obloquy that has been poured on this non-system, certainly since 1982, it has in practice served the world well in, first, the disinflation of the early 1980s and, secondly, by providing the stable environment for the longest inflation-free expansion in most Western countries. Yet there is good reason for believing that, however well the non-system has performed, if there is no acknowledged anchor for currencies, there are still dangers of runaway inflation.

The underlying rationale of the EMS/ERM was that, while we could not anchor to any commodity or gold, we could anchor to the currency with the best reputation and institutions to ensure stability ... the 'zone of stability' which was the original aim of the founders of the EMS. There is much to be said for this basic idea, *provided that the rate is absolutely fixed*. But, over the life of the EMS so far, exchange rates have not been fixed. They have wobbled in the band and moved at realignment. If the EMS/ERM rates had been really fixed, instead of pseudo-fixed, there would have been no possibility of profit from speculative capital movements, and indeed one of the main indictments of the EMS would have been null and void.

14

There is, however, a fundamental divide on the issue of fixed and pseudo-fixed exchange rates and monetary policy. I argue that absolutely fixed exchange rates are a good alternative to a free float. But then you must set up monetary institutions, such as a currency board, that are consistent with such fixity. There is no room for a monetary policy at all; in that sense monetary sovereignty is relinquished to Germany. This is a matter of both logic and fact, as is clear from the records of the many countries that have, over centuries, operated currency board systems. The only monetary role of a central bank is to exchange currencies at the fixed rate. I regard the pseudo-fixed system, with its wobbling in the band and propensity to leap to a new level on a 'realignment' session, as the worst of both worlds. Furthermore, pseudo-fixed exchange rates are accompanied by a pseudo monetary policy. Both are indeed half-baked.

Another disconcerting feature of the EMS/ERM arrangement is its dependence on the proper behaviour of the Bundesbank as an anchor. Historically, over more than three decades, the independent Bundesbank has behaved, if not impeccably, then certainly far better than any other central bank in defending the value of its currency. But, apart from the question whether that is good enough, legitimate doubts may be voiced about whether history is a reliable guide to future performance. Will the Bundesbank maintain its true independence and will it be able always to resist political pressures, such as those arising from the unification of the two Germanys, or those which emerge from international co-ordination similar to the Louvre accord?[2] One notes that the Federal Reserve Board, the other major independent central bank, did succumb to political pressures to inflate in the 1960s and 1970s. Inevitably the Bundesbank, just like the Fed, depends on the discretionary behaviour of people, rather than on the automatic rules of the old gold standard.

An Inflation-free Currency for Europe

Mr Lawson's idea that there should be competitive currencies to see which is the choice, not of the bureaucrats of Brussels, but of the private citizens of Europe is attractive. I believe, however, that there should be another competitor in the field — a currency which by its very constitution is neither inflationary nor deflationary. This would be a currency which maintains its constant and true value in terms of a defined basket of goods, such as the average consumption basket of European citizens. We shall call this currency the ECOM, to indicate that it is a European commodity money. Such a currency could be written into the constitution of Europe. It requires no central bank, only a bank of issue or a currency board.

If the ECOM is successful in its competition with other currencies, then it has a fair chance of being adopted as 'the' currency of Europe. Indeed, governments may agree to allow their currencies to be subsumed by it, initially through fixed exchange rates with the ECOM, and then entirely abolished in the adoption of the ECOM as the European currency. The great advantage of the ECOM is that it does not involve any surrender of sovereignty to a Central Bank of Europe, to the Bundesbank, or to the Brussels bureaucrats or European politicians. A Community state will surrender its monetary sovereignty to the principle of an inflation-free currency. That may well be a surrender which might be attractive to many of the Twelve.

And not only the Twelve. Since the departure from the old gold standard in 1914, the whole world has experienced persistent inflation (the only exceptional period being the years from 1929 to 1936). The world cannot and, indeed, should not return to the old gold standard or any version of the gold exchange and Bretton Woods systems. Gold is indeed a barbarous metal, of dubious provenance and subject to all the vagaries of technology and taste. A currency based on preserving constant the unit of account for a wide basket of commodities is much more desirable than a monetary unit linked to merely one precious metal. Nor do we need to keep stocks of commodities to operate the system. We can create paper assets which perform as surrogates for such commodities (unlike the old gold standard under which stocks of gold were *de rigeur*). The attractions are clear-cut. And if the Community were to make an obvious success of this ECOM, would not the United States, Canada, Japan, *et al.* be quick to follow? Just as the old gold standard arose around the pre-eminence of a liberal Britain, so might the ascent of a truly liberal Europe promote the new ECOM standard by the end of this century.

Such reflections are, of course, far beyond the economic consequences of Mr Lawson. But Mr Lawson can fairly claim to have opened wide (perhaps inadvertently) the debate on the monetary constitution for a liberal Europe. I hope that this book will add at least something to the debate.

IDEAS ON MONEY
AND EXCHANGE RATES

Monetarist approach

Exchange Rates as Allocators of Foreign Exchange

ONE OF THE MAIN jobs of the exchange rate is to ensure that people, both domestic residents and foreigners, are just willing to hold the stocks of money, be it pounds, dollars, marks or yen, that exist at any moment of time. Just as the price of a bond is such that people are just willing to hold the outstanding stock, so the exchange rate ensures that people are content to hold the various monies of the world. People will wish to hold a particular foreign money for many reasons: to pay for imports, to finance a visit, to buy assets, to make a remittance, or simply to hold as a speculation. These influences may change dramatically over time. But there is one ubiquitous influence that affects all these motives for holding foreign exchange: that is the price of the money or the rate of exchange. Like any other commodity, foreign exchange in general obeys the law of demand: the lower the price the larger the stock of foreign money people will wish to hold.

These motives for holding foreign exchange alter, usually quite unpredictably over time. Domestic droughts and disasters create a demand for foreign currency to finance imports. Discovery of some cornucopia of exportable minerals (such as gold or silver) creates for that country a ready supply of foreign currency — in other words, a foreign demand for the domestic currency.

The stock of money of each country is largely determined by the monetary authorities. It may be taken as approximately given. Then the problem is to allocate these existing stocks among the competing demands.

In a free-market system the authorities would simply allow freedom for any person or body to contract with any other, whether foreign or domestic, to sell foreign exchange at any mutually agreed price or exchange rate. Since the number of customers and suppliers is huge, the outcome is a very keen, competitive market exchange rate. This rate will move continuously to clear the market, and, often, instead of being called a free exchange rate, it is dubbed a 'flexible exchange rate'.[1]

Dirigisme and Interventions

There are other ways of doing this job of reconciling the demands with the existing stock. One way is to regulate the demands through some form of rationing. A common procedure is to regulate movements of capital and assets — that is, by 'capital controls'. But some countries practice more or less universal exchange controls and many limit the foreign currency and asset holdings of institutions. Although in some quarters there is a nostalgia for the days of fixed exchange rates supported by a battery of exchange controls, I believe that the vast majority of people are convinced that such instruments are inconsistent with the values of a liberal society.[2] Exchange controls are a viable if odious solution.

Another path by which demand and supply can be equated with a fixed exchange rate is through the monetary authorities of each country maintaining stocks of foreign exchange which they supply to the market when there is an excess demand, and which they take off the market when demand is less than supply at the fixed exchange rate. The problem is that the fixed exchange rate chosen may be or may become consistently too low or too high to match demand and supply. Then the monetary authorities will go on accumulating foreign exchange, if too low, or run out of stocks if too high. At best the operation of exchange equalisation through official intervention, as it is called, can only be a temporary respite and not a permanent solution. But intervention (we often miss out 'official') has many forms and ramifications. For most of this chapter we shall consider exchange rates in the absence of intervention, so that we can defer discussion of the forms of intervention to the end of the chapter.

Reconciliation Through Aggregate Demand[3]

The last method is for the authorities to affect the demand for foreign exchange by influencing the aggregate demand of the whole economy. Thus, with the exchange rate fixed, in order to reduce the demand for foreign money the authorities would attempt to reduce domestic prices relative to those of trading partners, so that people are weaned away from their demand for imports and foreign exchange, and the domestic currency is made more attractive for foreigners to hold. The main instrument for controlling domestic aggregate demand is monetary and perhaps fiscal policy (although in principle the tools of *dirigisme* can be employed also in macro-economic management). This method holds domestic monetary and fiscal policy hostage to the fixed exchange rate.

All these solutions have, of course, been employed at one time or another — often simultaneously in what the authorities would assert is a judicious mixture. But there is one central point. Clearly, since the exchange rate is the relative price of monies, any discussion of exchange rates must encompass an examination of monetary policies. The exchange rate is largely, but by no means wholly, a consequence of the monetary policies pursued by the monetary authorities. True, this rate may be maintained by official intervention, or defended by exchange controls. But the underlying free rate of exchange will be largely a consequence of relative monetary policies. Typically, the monetary authorities determine interest rates on the short-term money markets by using the power of the government as the biggest trader. Alternatively, monetary authorities fix the quantity of reserve money available to the banking system. But whatever the actual mechanism used, monetary policy determines the stock of money, and the rate of growth of money in the system.

If 'too much' money is created, then, like any other glut, the price of money will fall. People will try to reduce the amount of money they hold by spending it on goods and services and, if allowed by the authorities, on other (foreign) monies. Thus the domestic prices of goods and services will tend to rise. But this rise will be countered, in part, by foreign trade. Imports will increase and exports fall. The trade gap will open. To buy the additional imports more foreign currency is required, and there is a smaller supply from the reduced exports. The value of the foreign currency will increase; the domestic currency will depreciate. The over-expansion of money has reduced the value of the currency in terms of the size of the basket of goods it can buy on the home market and, through the exchange rate depreciation, on international markets.

Of course, factors other than monetary policy can affect the prices of goods and of currency. Boosts in real output, catastrophies, dislocations and recessions can affect the flow of goods and services. These effects change the flow of goods facing the monetary demand — the larger the flow the lower the price and the higher the value of the domestic currency. It is the increase in the supply of money relative to the increase in the supply of goods that is an important determinant of both prices and the exchange rate.

Confidence and Credibility

There is another much more nebulous set of influences that much affect exchange rates, particularly in the short run. They are to be summed up in the words, on the one hand, 'confidence' and 'credibility', and on the other, 'expectations' and 'uncertainty'. In his *General Theory*, Keynes argued that confidence was a main determinant of economic activity, but, realist that he was, he admitted that we did not know how to analyse it and its effects. Any market practitioner can feel in his bones whether confidence and credibility are high

21

or low. Among the things he will take into account are perceived consistency of policies, using whatever historical or parallel evidence seems relevant. I would claim that we have made *some* progress in analysing expectations of both monetary policy and exchange rates, and of their consequences.[4] But it is, I think, still true to say that our understanding of swings of confidence, and so forth, is very sketchy. As we shall see later, this is particularly unfortunate since much of the argument for joining the EMS/ERM and other fixed-exchange-rate systems hinges on the alleged accrual of credibility and confidence. This particularly applies, not so much to the goods market, but to the international market for financial assets — to which we shall shortly turn.

Real Exchange Rates (Goods)

In much of economics we are used to talking about money as a 'veil' over the important system of exchanges of *real* goods and services. Money serves as a transactions medium, but it is the underlying exchange of one good or service for another that is the real stuff of economic life. The exchange rate records merely the price of money in terms of a foreign money. It does not tell us the exchange rate between domestic and foreign goods and services.

If you are a casual reader or a pure economic theorist, the answer to this is obvious. Ignoring transport costs and trade barriers, it is ineluctable that the price of, say, a tonne of steel in Britain in pounds must be the same as the price of steel in Pittsburgh measured in dollars. If, *per contra*, the price in Britain were higher, then all steel buyers would rush to Pittsburgh, while the suppliers were deluging Britain with steel. The most delicate equilibrium requires the same real price. In the real world of transport and factoring costs, trade barriers, imperfect knowledge, sticky prices, etc., such an equilibrium is merely an abstraction. Prices, expressed in a common currency, do change over time. Indeed, these price changes are the essence of the process of adjustment to changing trading conditions.

They are so important that economists have defined them as the *real exchange rate* (RER) as distinct from the nominal exchange rate. As the nominal exchange rate measures the price of one money in terms of another, so the real exchange rate measures the price of traded goods in one country in terms of the price of traded goods in another country where the prices are both expressed in the same currency using the current nominal exchange rate. It looks simpler in algebraic form:

Real Exchange Rate (RER) = (£ Price in UK)/{(\$ Price in USA) (£ Value of \$)}

or

RER = {(\$Value of £) (£ Price in UK)}/(\$ Price in USA).

This expresses both numerator and denominator in sterling. As the ratio rises so the prices of goods in Britain increase relative to the prices in the United States. The UK becomes less competitive.[5] The real exchange rate ignores any change in price that is exactly counterbalanced by a change in the nominal exchange rate. Suppose, for example, that prices in the UK doubled whereas American prices remained constant; but if the nominal exchange rate changed so that we got only half as many dollars for the pound, the competitive conditions would remain the same. (One can think of it as shifting from a 100p to a 50p unit of account: the re-labelling does not affect the underlying realities.)

To illustrate the use of the real exchange rate (RER), let us imagine that for some exogenous reason the world's taste shifts from goods that Britain produces (scotch whisky) to foreign products (champagne). The real exchange rate needs to fall to induce the world to buy the flows of scotch and champagne. Assume that Britain is a small part of the world market for champagne so that the dollar price of champagne does not change. Then one way this fall in the RER can be achieved is by reducing the sterling price of scotch, holding the nominal exchange rate constant. An alternative is for sterling to depreciate against the dollar while holding the two prices constant. And there are obviously many alternatives between (and indeed outside) these two solutions. A flexible exchange rate gives another degree of freedom in the adjustment of real exchange rates for goods.

In the theoretical world of champagne and scotch, the prices one uses are obvious. Alas, this does not carry over to the real bread-and-butter world. There are many possible theoretical RERs, depending on the questions one is examining. And there are many limitations on the measurement of RERs due, primarily, to the limited data available on price movements. Since the purpose of this book is to examine the process of monetary policy on exchange rates and inflation, it is natural to define the RER in terms of the price indices of *traded goods* or tradeable goods. Rough approximations to these can be found in the wholesale price indices or producer price indices. But there are many problems of interpretation.

Real Exchange Rates (Capital)

The relative prices of goods are only part, indeed to many the least important part, of the story. The main 'commodities' that flow across national frontiers are financial instruments, such as deposits, bills, CDs, bonds, and so on. The flows of foreign exchange business connected with capital exports and imports far exceed (perhaps by a factor of 50) those concerned with goods and services. The fundamental idea of the real, as distinct from the nominal, exchange rate also applies to these capital movements. But financial instruments are different from goods and services. With a tonne of steel the price paid is the only monetary transaction. Financial instruments, however, normally involve future money flows defined in a particular currency. These include not merely the interest or dividend payments but also the return of principal. Thus it is not only the current or 'spot' rate of exchange that affects the relative price (the RER) but also expected future values of *the exchange rate*.

Forward Markets

This problem of differing maturities of payments, however, is solved if there are suitable forward markets for foreign exchange. If a one-year deposit in dollars yields 8 per cent and a one-year deposit in sterling yields 15 per cent, then, in the absence of transactions costs, it will pay *any* investor to put his money·in sterling if he can get a guarantee to buy dollars (sell sterling) in one year's time at less than a 7 per cent premium (7 per cent discount) on the current spot rate. This rush into sterling will stop when the total rate of return (that is to say, the interest rate minus any loss on buying one-year forward dollars) on sterling deposits is equal to that on dollar deposits. This implies that, in equilibrium, there must be *covered-interest-rate parity*, that is, for one year:

> Interest on sterling = Interest on dollars *plus* forward dollar premium

> or

> Interest on dollars = Interest on sterling *minus* forward dollar premium.

This knife-edge equilibrium ensures that there is no incentive for switching from one currency deposit to another.

Covered Interest Parity — Reality and Causation

The covered-interest-rate-parity equation is a pure or theoretical case. It is analogous to the pure case of Pittsburgh steel with no transactions or transport costs, perfect knowledge and no trade restrictions. Then, just as the price of steel must be the same in each country, so in this case the rate of return which one gets on the same sum of money must also be the same in each country.[6] But there is much more reason to take the case of the equality of return on money as much closer to reality than the case of steel and most other goods. Interest rates move with far more alacrity than the prices of goods. No stickiness there. For money, transactions costs are much smaller, and transport costs are virtually zero. In free markets, therefore, the covered-interest parity will be a close approximation to reality.

The equation does not imply anything about *causation*. It merely states what must rule in equilibrium. It does not tell us how that equality is brought about, or how interest rates, spot exchange rates and forward premia or discounts interact with one another. For those causal relationships one must look at the underlying relationships of demand and supply. Whatever story we tell, however, must be consistent continuously with the covered parity principle. The covered parity rule does tell us that obvious, but often ignored, fact that, in a free market, a government cannot simultaneously truly fix the exchange rate and at the same time vary interest rates as required for an independent monetary policy.

One might perhaps expect that the forward markets would give an accurate guide on the realised path of exchange rates. The markets reflect a sort of consensus of views about the expected path of the rate, and it is often said that markets are efficient in using all the relevant available information in making forecasts of the future. An interesting point, however, about the foward markets for foreign exchange is that they are poor predictors of performance.[7] Indeed, knowledge of the foward market values is of no use in predicting the future actual path of spot exchange rates. In fact, the current spot rate is a better predictor of future spot rates than is the forward rate. These results are not really surprising. If there really were information in the forward rates about the actual path, then that information would be the source of profit; everyone would realise it and so drive the spot and future rates to values where all the profitable information has been leeched out, leaving only the dross in the forward values. Nevertheless, these forward markets do provide an invaluable way of hedging currency risks or speculating on the outcome. As we shall argue, such markets enable us to overcome many of the alleged disadvantages of a float.

The Effective Exchange Rate

Up to now, the discussion has been simplified by supposing that there is only one exchange rate between domestic residents and a homogeneous mass called foreigners — between us and them. In the real world there are about 170 countries, almost all of which have their own currency. Thus there are some 160 exchange rates between sterling and other currencies. Obviously some, such as the US dollar and the Deutschemark, are much more important than others, such as the kwatcha or cedi. In order to get a simple measure of the movements in the nominal exchange rate, *vis à vis* all other countries, one needs some system of weighting in order to get an average exchange rate that reflects the importance of the countries. The best weighting system would be one that reflected the number and size of foreign exchange transactions in each currency. But, so far as I am aware, no such weighting system is used — probably because of the difficulty of getting reliable comprehensive data on foreign exchange transactions.

Instead the authorities have devised what is called an 'effective exchange rate' which weights each constituent foreign exchange rate by the total amount of trade between Britain and that particular country. The effective exchange rate (EER) is in fact the trade-weighted exchange rate, and is reported as an index number. The real effective exchange rate (REER) is calculated in the same way.

For most of the discussion in the following chapters, I shall refer to *the* sterling exchange rate without going into the complexities of the effective rate. But it should be understood that I am referring to the EER or the REER.

The Many Jobs Done by the Exchange Rate

From the discussion of goods and money and capital markets as well as from the complexities of many countries, it seems that the exchange rate performs a myriad of tasks. But it is useful to summarise them under two general headings:

First, the exchange rate moves to equilibrate the demand and supply of traded goods and services. Although for most primary commodities, such as grain, oils and metals, prices move speedily to clear the market, in manufactured goods there is usually some considerable stickiness in their prices. They move sluggishly in response to market forces. The exchange rate in a free market, however, moves with alacrity and speedily signals and eliminates the shortages and surpluses on the goods markets (but not on the labour market!). At the same time the exchange rate must ensure that, along with interest rates, there is a sufficient attraction to capital flows to finance the deficit on the current account of the balance of payments. The net capital inflow, from dollars to pounds, must be just enough to balance the whole account.

Second, the exchange rate must be such that the existing quantities of non-interest bearing money in both the domestic and foreign countries be willingly held. If there is too much of the domestic currency relative to the foreign currency, then the domestic currency will decline in value in terms of the foreign currency (that is, it will depreciate). One might go further and argue that it is also the critical factor that induces people willingly to hold the existing quantities of financial assets denominated in, respectively, the domestic and foreign currency. But in the case of financial assets generally, as distinct from non-interest bearing money, one must also take account of the yield in one currency on such assets. It is clear, however, that the exchange rate does a most important job in ensuring that people willingly hold the existing stocks of financial assets in the specific currency denominations of their choice.

Like other phenomena in economics, this simple price of one currency in terms of another does an enormously complex job of co-ordinating millions — perhaps even trillions — of decisions about producing and consuming goods, adjusting portfolios, investment, etc. The free price system is a wondrous mechanism that can do all these things through the self-regarding behaviour of individuals. The millions of individuals rarely see one another, probably do not understand each other's language, and may even be highly antagonistic. Yet, through the price system, they achieve an immense harmony of co-operation and co-ordination. It is also clear that highly managed exchange rate and planning systems that eschew the use of free price adjustments have been dismal failures — as the experience of Eastern Europe and the Soviet Union attests.

Long-Run PPP and Short-Run Dynamics

Yet our understanding of the workings of the free-market system is, to put it mildly, imperfect. In the field of monetary policy and exchange rates it is particularly important to be clear about what we do and what we do not know. Of course we step on much disputed territory. What follows is very much a personal interpretation. This is based on my reading of theory, the evidence, and direct observation.

First and most important of all is that, in the *long run*, the purchasing power parities of currencies (PPP) must be roughly equal. Exchange rates must adjust to reflect the differences in the price levels. Thus a one-shot increase of the money supply will give rise to an increase in the price level and a depreciation in the exchange rate — both in the long run. Similarly, an expansion of monetary growth, relative to those of our trading partners, which is expected to persist will give rise to a long-run continual depreciation of sterling.[8]

There are many pertinent examples of this 'long-run' rule. For example, the long-run depreciation of sterling against the Deutschemark and the dollar attests to the fact that the monetary policies of Germany and the United States have been less expansionary and that their inflation rates have been, on the average, lower than those in the United Kingdom.

I believe that there is a broad agreement among economists that we can be fairly confident of the long-run effects of monetary policy on the price level and on exchange rates.

The former goes up and the latter down, more or less proportionately. But there is much less agreement on the *short-term* dynamics of the adjustment process — again, both in monetary economics and in exchange rate dynamics.

The basic problem is that, in the short run, there are many complexities and effects which are difficult to model and impossible to control. In the weekly or monthly adjustments, for example, expectations and uncertainty must play a dominant role. Rumour and report of political events can play havoc with markets. Furthermore, short-term movements in output, stickiness of prices, excess capacity will all have important, even dominant, effects in weekly or monthly movements.

Overshooting

One commonly accepted account of the transitional reaction of exchange rates to changes in monetary growth suggests that, far from rising monotonically to its new equlibrium value, the nominal exchange rate will far overshoot its long-run target, but in the long run it will return to its PPP level.[9] The rationalisation is most easily seen if we first assume that total real output is fixed throughout. An expansion of the money supply will have the effect of depressing interest rates. Everyone will expect that prices will rise and that there will have to be a corresponding devaluation in the long run. But the fall in interest rates will give rise, in the very short term, to a capital flight which will in turn cause a sudden and sharp devaluation. The devaluation will cease when domestic residents can secure an overall rate of return, that is, interest plus expected appreciation of the currency, equal to that which they can gain abroad. In order to provide this expected appreciation, the sharp fall in the exchange rate must be sufficient to take it *below* the long-run equilibrium value. Then all asset holders can look forward to an appreciation of the domestic currency *up to* the long-run equilibrium. In short, the spot exchange rate must fall below its new long-run equilibrium path, so that the future appreciation of the exchange rate will compensate for the initial fall in interest rates.[10]

A quite crucial feature of this story is that the prices in the markets for manufactured goods and labour adjust much more slowly than prices in the markets for assets and in foreign exchange.[11] The increase in demand due to the monetary expansion will be generated not only through the lower domestic interest rates but also through the devaluation. Since the sticky prices are fixed in the short run, this implies that the nominal devaluation is also a *real* devaluation. But prices will then increase over the adjustment period, and both the nominal and the real exchange rate will rise. Indeed, over this period one will observe increasing prices and an appreciating exchange rate — exactly the opposite of the long-run adjustment!

This neat picture is somewhat obfuscated if one allows for potential movements in output. There is some evidence that a monetary expansion boosts real output during the shortish run — between some six months and perhaps up to 18 months before it dies away and becomes negative. This expansion will tend to reduce the fall in interest rates, perhaps even increase them, and so dampen the overshoot after six months or so of the adjustment period. But the 6-18 months' boost to output will then be reversed.[12] This will produce yet another downward force on interest rates and an appreciation of the spot exchange rate lagged at least some 18 months behind the original monetary injection. Yet another late overshoot is possible, which is likely to occur just at the time when the sluggish prices are at last starting to move up.

Of course, any reader having got this far will conclude either that economists who produce models which capture this dynamic process must be fiendishly clever or that such economists do not know what they are talking about. Both are true.

However plausible this account of the dynamics of adjustment, it is far from being a reliable, tested proposition.

Casual knowledge suggests that exchange rates have fluctuated more than monetary policy and the overshoot hypothesis may be one of the explanations. But there are many more influences on the dynamics of exchange rates, as we know from the fact of their short-run unpredictability. I would be inclined, however, to regard the overshooting phenomenon as something to look for but not something to rely upon.

An Alternative — Short-Run Perversity

This sceptical view is supported by an alternative view of the short-run adjustment mechanism, which seems to me to have just as much plausibility as the overshooting hypothesis. Suppose, *per contra*, that domestic prices — such as the prices of real estate, café services and, above all, the prices of commodities — do respond rather quickly to the increased demand. Let us then begin again with a monetary expansion at home. Instead of looking at the path of equilibrium through the need to induce people to hold existing stocks of financial assets, let us examine instead the *flow* equilibrium through exports and imports, brought about by an excess domestic aggregate demand.

With a domestic supply response which is not elastic enough, in the short run at least, to assuage the growth of domestic demand, the only way to satisfy the demand is through decreased net exports. In order to reduce exports the sterling price of those exportable goods, *relative to the prices of non-traded goods*, such as houses and haircuts, must be increased. The deficit on the current balance of payments will therefore increase. And in order to ensure such an increase in the overseas deficit, the real exchange rate must *appreciate* during the adjustment phase. Thus, the (albeit transitory) movement of the exchange rate is perverse.

This is exactly the opposite of the sticky-price-overshooting theory. In the long run, however, the stories converge. In the appreciation case, the deficit on the current balance is eventually eliminated, via a transitory surplus, and the economy settles down at higher prices but at a restored relative price of tradeable to non-tradeable goods. It all comes out the same in the end.

But this should be of little comfort to those who seek to track the short-term oscillations of the exchange rate — or indeed to those who seek to hang the economy on such shifting values. I suspect that most professional economists in the field would be prepared to defend the sticky-price-overshooting version of the adjustment process. The slow reaction of the prices in markets for manufactured goods, compared with the speedy reaction in the markets for financial assets, is a common theme of most accounts of the adjustment process. Yet there is no theoretical reason why this should be the case. Nor has there been any extensive empirical investigation of the issue of price flexibility. Casual observation suggests that the prices of goods, particularly food, are highly flexible, often reflecting daily or weekly oscillations in supply. Similarly, no-one can be in doubt about the boom-and-bust flexibility in the housing market. The reader may well reflect that this flexible price model tells a story which is rather similar to the experience of Britain in 1987-89; this is a theme I will take up again in Chapter 6.

Exchange Rates as a Monetary Thermometer?

As a result of this discussion, one might concede that, in the short run, the nominal exchange rate is of dubious utility as an indicator of the appropriate monetary policy. This conclusion should occasion little surprise. Just as we know little about the short-run adjustments of the economy to a monetary expansion, so we know perhaps even less about the oscillations in the exchange rate. The exchange rate is one of the main channels through which the effects of a monetary expansion are tranmitted to the rest of the economy and to foreign countries. And it is above all a monetary phenomenon. Our lack of knowledge of the dynamic adjustment paths of prices, real output, interest rate structures, etc., *should* be mirrored in exchange rates. And so it is.

This discussion of the principles of exchange rate adjustment has ignored, or taken as constant, many of the important determinants of exchange rates in practice. Changes in the weather, in political prospects, in technology, in the marginal profitability of domestic fixed capital formation, in thrift, and in expectations and confidence all impinge, often quite dramatically, on exchange rates. Even after the event, it is difficult or often impossible, neatly to attribute an exchange rate movement to its causes. It is quite impossible to do so for current movements in exchange rates. For example, in 1987-88 the upward pressure on sterling *vis à vis* the Deutschemark did not indicate that Britain was enduring a monetary squeeze compared with Germany; the contrary was the case, for reasons which we shall go into later (Chapter 5).

Fixed Rates and Stability

It has been suggested that, by adopting whatever monetary policy is necessary to assure fixed exchange rates, compared with any alternative régime, the economy will be much more stable and avoid sharp variations in output and inflationary or deflationary pressure. Protagonists of this view lean heavily on the assertion that confidence will be much greater under a fixed exchange rate régime than under any alternative arrangement.[13] As argued above, there are a great many aspects to the concept of confidence and certainly there is no tested theory which tells us how to analyse it. Statements about it reflect largely the taste of the asserter. There are, of course, a myriad of subsidiary assumptions underlying any such assertion about, for example, the soaring confidence that would allegedly ensue if Britain joined the ERM, albeit a pseudo régime. We shall defer discussion of these assumptions, but it is worthwhile reflecting at this stage on the efficacy of a fixed exchange rate régime.

What is required of a monetary and exchange rate régime is, I think, broadly agreed. We would like a stable and low (say, 0 to 3 per cent) rate of inflation, and we would like a high and stable growth rate with only sufficient unemployment to enable the market to work efficiently. From our discussion of exchange rates and monetary policy, it seems unlikely that, even if the reserve currency to which the currency was fixed behaved in the most immaculate manner, a fixed exchange rate régime would promote such conditions. For example, if the overshooting hypothesis is true, then any accidental monetary expansion would, under a fixed régime, require a very large short-term increase in interest rates to offset the power of the overshoot.[14] This increase would then lead to a great contraction in the rate of growth of the money supply, with an attendant recession to follow. If, however, the perverse model is true, then any accidental monetary expansion would be followed by pressure for an exchange rate appreciation, which must be eventually reversed. Such paths are hardly stable or secure.

The Fundamental Equilibrium Real Exchange Rate (FERER)

Clearly, one of the main ideas of a fix is that, once done, it is possible simply to let the system run on a sort of auto-pilot. However, the system critically depends on getting the fix right. As Churchill discovered, it was disastrous to get the wrong value to fix upon. In order to assist statesmen in this process, economists have tried not merely defining but actually specifying an underlying equilibrium rate. The value beloved of the fixers is the fundamental equilibrium real exchange rate (FERER). The idea is that there is an underlying exchange rate which, ignoring transitory random variations brought about by swings in confidence and expectations, etc., would give rise to a deficit just sufficient to balance the capital flow required to exploit the greater profitability of capital in the receiving country. Somehow the FERER is the 'right' rate.

I think that virtually all economists and many others carry around some idea of an appropriate rate. Yet it is impossible to define one that is useful for policy purposes. Of course, we

35

would all begin with some idea about PPP in order to get an appropriate figure in the current balance, so that there is suitable room for the desired capital flows. Such a concept would, however, ignore many realities of economic life — and to the peril of the policy-maker. For example, suppose there is a penumbra of political uncertainty, say a left-wing take-over with capital and exchange controls in train, then this would have a dominant effect on the market exchange rate, allowing for capital flight on an unpredictable timetable. It is clearly impossible to put such ideas into the FERER.

If it is difficult to define an operationally useful FERER, it is quite impossible to make any meaningful measures of the concept. We have only sketchy ideas about the demand and supply conditions in international trade, as is obvious from the large errors which forecasters make in their predictions. Virtually nothing at all can be forecast about the profitability of capital in Britain and her trading partners, and the job of defining a neutral monetary policy and the associated interest rates is quite beyond any mortal's abilities. Ignorance rules.

It is not surprising, therefore, that the most eminent economists have ventured completely different views about the appropriate movement of nominal exchange rates. In 1988, for example, Martin Feldstein argued that the yen should appreciate against the dollar in order to eliminate a large US deficit, but, at the same time, Ronald McKinnon (with considerable support from the *Wall Street Journal*) was urging a devaluation of the yen in order to return to purchasing power parity. In the famous Louvre Agreement (February 1987) it was asserted that the dollar-yen and dollar-Deutschemark were 'consistent with the underlying fundamentals', although they required enormous intervention to keep them in place.

This suggests that, even if we knew how to define the FERER, we do not know how to measure it and use it operationally. And there is great danger in using simple calculations of PPP to decide on directions of exchange rate

Figure 1:
The US-UK Real Exchange Rate, 1869-1989

(Index: 1980 = 100)

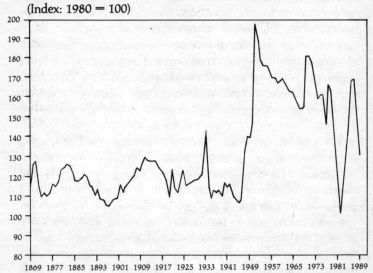

Source: J. A. Dorn and W. A. Niskanen (eds.) , *Dollars, Deficits and Trade*, Washington
DC: Cato Institute, 1989, p. 175.

movement towards equilibrium. Substantial variations in
PPP can take place, and indeed have taken place over the
years since the Second World War (see Figure 1). Such
deviations can persist for a long time. (Indeed, today all
frequent transatlantic travellers are convinced that $160 in
Washington buys much more than £100 sterling in
London — and has done for some time.) One should beware
of using any simple PPP calculations as a guide to deter-
mining what are the 'fundamentals'.

The impossibility of defining and fixing the FERER is
simply an illustration of the general proposition that it is
impossible to fix any set of equilibrium prices. But this is no
clinching argument against fixing the nominal exchange rate.
It is perfectly possible to fix the nominal exchange rate
and to allow inflation, and the consequent effects on
activity, freely to adjust and validate the nominal rate. This is

37

the underlying rationale of truly fixed exchange rate systems.

Intervention — Unsterilized and Sterilized

The discussion of official intervention, one of the four ways of securing a reconciliation of demand and supply in foreign exchange markets, was deferred while we considered the various other equilibrating mechanisms. Now we consider the direct involvement of government or central bank in the market.

The simplest form of intervention, unsterilized, is for the government to sell or buy foreign exchange *in order to affect the rate*, with no concomitant open-market operations in the bond market.[15] Thus if the Bank of England sells pounds and increases its reserves of dollars, this would be intervention against sterling and in support of the dollar. The important point is that the private sector would acquire more pounds. This foreign exchange transaction would increase the sterling money supply of the United Kingdom. This will eventually increase the price level. Thus the selling of sterling for dollars is simply a way of increasing the money supply. Instead of buying long-dated bonds, as in normal open-market operations, the Bank buys dollar balances.

For the most part, however, governments want to intervene *only* to influence the exchange rate. They may be quite content with their monetary stance and wish to confine effects to the foreign exchange market. Thus they wish to *sterilize* the intervention and offset any effects on monetary policy. If the target of monetary policy is the growth rate of some monetary aggregate, then in the sale of sterling example, sterilization would take the form of open-market sales of a sufficiently large number of long-dated gilts in order to mop up the sterling created by the intervention. The money created by intervention is taken back in the gilt sales. The market ends up with the same amount of money, increased holdings of gilts and reduced holdings of foreign exchange.

Sterilization — Forms and Effects

This definition of sterilization, although much used in theoretical work, is not the usual one used by central bankers in their actual operations. For the most part central banks control short-term interest rates as their main instrument of monetary policy. Thus it is natural to define sterilization in terms of *maintaining the short-term interest rates unchanged*. In the Bank of England operations, for example, the Bank supplies or subtracts from the market daily just sufficient funds to maintain the short-term interest rates thought to be appropriate for monetary policy. When a substantial intervention, such as selling of sterling, takes place, the Bank mops up any excess that appears in the daily money markets to threaten the maintenance of the interest rate. In that sense, therefore, the Bank always sterilizes — up to the point at which it is decided to vary the short-term interest rate.[16] When interest-rate changes are associated with intervention, then it is unsterilized.

But the important question is: *Does sterilized intervention work*? Does it really affect exchange rates substantially while maintaining unchanged the monetary stance? From experience, there is no doubt that sterilized intervention does have some effect in the *short run*. The immediate effect of foreign currency sales appears on the markets and probably has some effect on the market's expectations. However, it is very likely that this effect lasts only for a short time — days rather than weeks. But, as Michael Mussa says:

> 'There is good reason to doubt ... that pure (i.e. sterilized) official intervention can have a significant effect on the long-run behaviour of exchange rates ... When the market becomes persuaded that the authorities are attempting to maintain a disequilibrium exchange rate, the magnitude of intervention required to sustain the rate rapidly grows to enormous proportions.'[17]

In view of what happened in Britain in early 1988, it is easy to appreciate Mussa's point.

In short, sterilized intervention is an instrument useful only for playing short-run games with the market. (In my view this is unseemly behaviour for a central bank, but many regard it as a useful weapon in the bank's fearsome armoury.) It cannot have any long-run effect on exchange rates. The very failure of sterilized intervention, however, has its effects on monetary policy. When sterilized intervention fails to shore up, or keep down, an exchange rate, then the authorities are tempted to, and often do, change monetary policy. As we shall see, this is what Mr Lawson did in May of 1988.

MONEY AND EXCHANGE RATES IN PRACTICE

Bretton Woods didn't work well
— & couldn't have

The High Keynesian Consensus, 1945-69

SOME THIRTY YEARS AGO, when I began to work on monetary economics, it was generally thought that money and monetary policy had little or no effect on the price level or the rate of inflation. In those days of high Keynesianism (or the 'New Economics' as it was called in Kennedy's United States), it was thought that inflation was largely determined by the extent of unemployment and the fiscal deficit. Low unemployment would ensure that any fiscal stimulus from an expansion in the fiscal deficit would generate increases in prices rather than increases in output, inflation rather than growth. If, however, there was a lot of unemployment, then any fiscal stimulus would increase employment and output with little or no effect on prices and inflation. Most inflations were caused by 'cost-push' factors such as trade unions demanding too big a wage increase, or greedy business misusing their market power to push up prices, or unconcerned foreigners increasing import prices.

In the list of *dramatis personae*, money was merely a bit player. The authoritative Radcliffe Report (1959) had said unequivocally that the quantity of money did not matter very much because the velocity of circulation could be 'infinite'. Lord Kaldor opined that the role of money was simply to maintain 'orderly [financial] markets'. He likened it to his trousers which, he said, as he got fatter he let out the seams, rather than go on a diet. With such compelling imagery, the main point was that monetary policy should be accommodating so that the really important levers of fiscal policy, and the various direct controls over investment, etc., were appropriately effective.

The policy objective of high Keynesianism was to pursue near-full employment by ensuring just enough fiscal stimulus that would at the same time guarantee there would be no inflation. The margin of the small army of unemployed would ensure that wage push would never get out of hand, and although business might exert its latent monopoly power or foreigners might demand more for their wares, such effects could not go on year after year. Competition, both domestic and international, would exert a discipline on such inflationary forces.

Foreign trade served as a temporary safety valve. Any overstimulus of fiscal policy would be partially dissipated in an expansion of net imports to meet the excess demand. The resulting deficit on the current balance of payments would absorb at least part of the incipient inflationary pressure. Clearly, this was strictly a temporary respite since one could run a persistent deficit only if foreigners were willing to lend enough money to finance it.

Foreign Exchange Rate Régimes

Now we ought to look, at least superficially, at the foreign exchange régime. In order to sort out the various strands in the argument, it is convenient first to discuss what would happen if there were no restrictions at all in foreign exchange transactions. In these years Britain was on a pseudo-fixed or pegged exchange rate and not a really fixed one. There had been two devaluations in 1947 and 1967. But if Britain had been on a *really fixed* exchange rate, then, provided that no doubts arose about the credit-worthiness of the government, Britain would have been able to finance these deficits by borrowing at interest rates little different from those of the lenders (say, the United States). For if a pound *always* buys, and is always expected with complete confidence to buy 2.40 dollars, then the interest rates in Britain must be the same as those in the United States.[1]

Under such conditions, namely, no exchange or capital controls and absolute confidence in the maintenance of the dollar value of sterling, interest rates and monetary policy were out of the hands of the British government. Thus any inflationary pressure, whether generated by cost-push trade unions or natural calamities, could not be countered by a tighter monetary policy. Only the instruments of fiscal policy were available.

The effectiveness of fiscal instruments, such as changes in taxation and public expenditure, appeared to be becoming weaker and even perverse during the 1960s and into the 1970s.[2] The powerful instruments of monetary policy, however, had not been entirely emasculated by the Bretton Woods system of fixed exchange rates. First, the authorities rationed, with various degrees of tightness, foreign exchange (dollars) to the residents. The authorities simply did not allow one to switch out of sterling into dollars, except for limited amounts and with good reason ('good reason' did not include expectation of a higher yield!). Second, and most important, was that sterling was never inflexibly fixed. Sterling was a pseud in Bretton Woods. The likelihood of a devaluation, particularly high at various periods (for example, the Suez crisis in 1956, and from 1963 to the eventual devaluation in 1967), was always an ambient risk. The size of the foreign exchange balances and other realisable foreign assets was an imperfect but useful indicator of the risk of devaluation.

Capital Flows and the Demise of Bretton Woods

Thus in practice there was room for Britain to pursue its own monetary policy, primarily through fixing interest rates and controlling monetary expansion by various forms of credit rationing. It is ironic that it was the probability of devaluation that enabled a member to pursue monetary policies that made it possible to stay in the system. In the 1950s and through the early years of the 1960s, private capital flows were rather small; governments were the main money movers. By the end of the 1960s, however, there was a substantial free-booting Eurodollar market in London which dwarfed the official flows. Thus while, up to, say, 1965 it had been possible for governments to help one another stay at the fixed parities by lending one another sums of foreign currency (as in the case of the United States' loan to Britain in 1956), and these loans dominated the market, after 1965 government funds were eclipsed by private flows. And the incentive for the private sector meant, of course, that private funds flowed against the official tide, eventually swamping it.

The most telling demonstration of the power of private capital flows to upset the desire of governments to hold exchange rate parities was in sterling's devaluation of 1967. The Labour government of 1964 inherited the pre-election monetary fling of Maudling (the Tory chancellor). The inflationary genie was out of the bottle, and although Mr Wilson tried every trick, including high interest rates, draconian credit controls, a budgetary squeeze, stringent restrictions on foreign exchange, and even an import surcharge, the flight of private capital (led by the 'gnomes of Zurich', according to Mr Wilson) could not be offset by intergovernmental borrowings. Sterling had to go in November 1967, from $2.80 to $2.40. Even so doubts persisted whether it had gone far enough; and the hallowed Bretton Woods system was essentially a casualty of free capital movements.

Myths and Reality in Bretton Woods

Much nostalgia has been lavished on the Bretton Woods system.[3] It is said that it provided a great stability and low inflation during the 24 years or so (1947-71) it was in operation. This misses important realities. First, the Bretton Woods system did not really become *effective* until the end of the 1950s. Before then all the major currencies were inconvertible, so private capital movements were precluded and, for example, many of Britain's old colonies were saddled with sterling balances which they could only use at the discretion of the British government. And clearly,

44

even before 1967, everyone knew that the second most important currency was in turmoil. After 1967 one saw essentially the end of gold convertibility in the two-tier gold window, where the United States would honour convertibility, albeit reluctantly, only for central banks. The system was moribund and then died in 1971. So the Bretton Woods system really lasted at most some 10 years. It is indeed ironic that the great inflation of 1972-75 was generated under the Bretton Woods system, whereas the great disinflation of the 1980s was achieved when all the major currencies were floating.[4]

The story of Bretton Woods is one of the major reserve currency, the dollar, and the minor reserve currency, sterling, beginning by being undervalued.[5] Gradually, however, expansionary monetary policies took their toll. The United States increased its rate of monetary growth from the early 1960s and the great inflation got under way. The dollar shortage, which had prevented convertibility throughout much of the 1950s, became a dollar glut. At its fixed parities, with respect to European currencies, the dollar had become overvalued. At its gold parity, there was a big excess demand for the contents of Fort Knox. So in the last act of the Bretton Woods saga, the two reserve currencies ended the 1960s as overvalued and unwanted. The United States, which had been accused of dragging the world into recession in the 1950s, was then accused, quite rightly, of exporting its inflation through the Bretton Woods system.

Alternatives Foregone?

There were alternatives to floating, none of them very palatable, however. One possible (Churchillian) solution would have been for the United States to pursue a persistent deflationary policy by reducing monetary growth to, say, zero. It is doubtful if this could have been done from 1971 onwards without substantial dislocation and unemployment. The United States would certainly have been accused of exporting its *recession* to the rest of the world. Another

45

solution would have been for Germany, for example, to pursue inflationary policies to reduce the differential between the dollar and the mark. But Germany and many other countries were adamant about the need to avoid domestic inflation and resented importing inflation from the United States. Why should Germany pay for the mismanagement of the United States?

It is interesting to reflect on whether Bretton Woods would have survived if the United States had not inflated in the 1960s. With responsible behaviour on the part of the major reserve currency country, could not the Bretton Woods system have survived to this day? I very much doubt whether it could. The US inflation merely hastened a death which was inevitable. The first reason is the burgeoning private capital flows which increasingly won the battle against official intervention. The second reason is that fixed exchange rates could never have taken the enormous strain caused by the oil price and other shocks of the 1970s. Lastly, fixed exchange rates generate these kinds of tensions between the participating governments. When the reserve currency is too strong, its partners accuse it of inducing a recession, whereas when it is too weak, it will be condemned as an inflationist. And no currency is ever just right.

Floating and Monetarism, 1971-90

Just as there is no pure fixity of exchange rates, so there is no pure floating. In a pure float the government would not undertake transactions in foreign exchange that were outside the normal processes of government taxation and spending and designed to affect the value of the currency. Even the most 'hands-off' policy will often consider the timing of taxation dates and payment schedules in order to smooth the market process. It is convenient, however, to consider the pure float as a theoretical category since one can analyse it much more easily. Most countries, however, pursued what was dubbed a 'dirty float'. Governments intervened in foreign exchange markets, sometimes buying their own currency in order to prevent a reduction (or to secure a rise) in its value, or selling it in order to prevent a rise (or to secure a fall). (Nor did they restrict intervention merely to their own currency. Indeed, if one has enough money, anyone can intervene in any traded currency to influence its value. But clearly the game is really restricted to governments which can dip liberally into the pockets of taxpayers to spend on their wizard wheezes.)

The unpegging of exchange rates meant that countries had much more latitude to pursue independent monetary policies. Under complete freedom from exchange controls, sterling interest rates could exceed US interest rates if the value of the pound were expected to decrease in terms of dollars. For example, if the pound were expected to depreciate by 5 percentage points against the dollar over the year, then 12-month interest rates of, say, 14 per cent in London and 9 per cent in New York could happily co-exist. The average expectation of return on a sterling or dollar asset would be the same.

Consequences of Floating

This is the first, and perhaps the most important, consequence of free exchange rates. It enables Britain to pursue a monetary policy which does not have slavishly to follow that of the major monetary power, whether the United States or Germany. British monetary growth can be determined by domestic conditions, and the appropriate interest rates will emerge, together with the expected change in the value of sterling, on the market. Or, alternatively, British short-term interest rates can be fixed by government operations in the money markets to produce the monetary conditions which it believes are appropriate. One should beware, however, of claiming too much for floating rates. In the short run, there has been substantial interdependence — in, for example, the transitory reactions to the OPEC oil price increases of 1973 and 1979. Floating does not insulate us completely from short-run shocks. It helps but it is no panacea. For the *long*

47

run, however, there is considerable evidence that floating rates have given the independence of monetary policies, movements in prices and interest rates which one would expect. And in the control of inflation this is the critical test.[6]

Another important consequence of floating, however dirty, has been that it enabled countries to reduce or eliminate controls on both the flows of goods and of money and capital. With no desperate need to defend an exchange rate parity, there was no need for the desperate measures which Mr Wilson had been induced to deploy in 1964-68. In Britain the floating rate eventually enabled Mrs Thatcher to abolish all exchange controls, both overt and covert, in 1979-80. Similarly, the United States found it no longer desirable to employ the battery of capital controls which it had introduced in the 1960s. One may contrast this with the persistence of exchange controls and the growth of trade restrictions in the EMS from 1979 to 1987. This does not, of course, mean that floating countries are bound to adopt more liberal régimes than fixed countries. Floating removes merely many of the incentives for *dirigisme*.

Alternatives to Floating

It is instructive for us in Britain to examine dispassionately what would have happened in the last decade if the world had been on some alternative régime. All the alternatives that have been suggested are variants of the Bretton Woods type of 'fixed but flexible' or 'stable but adjustable' pegs. From November 1982, the economy of the United States embarked on a sustained non-inflationary expansion. Both a very large trade deficit and a massive nominal and real appreciation of the dollar ensued. The deficit provided the stimulus to the rest of the OECD countries and pulled them out of the slump. It also allowed a considerable capital inflow into the United States in response to the high profitability of investment engendered, in part, by tax reductions.

If the United States had been constrained by a Bretton Woods type of system to keep the dollar down at its 1979 level (in effective terms), this would have required a massive injection of dollars into the world monetary system. It would have produced a monster of an inflation which would have destroyed confidence in an even more devastating manner than the inflation of the 1960s and early 1970s. It is likely that the system would have broken down with resort to controls and protectionism. Back to the *dirigisme* of the 1930s!

I suspect that it is widely accepted that there was no really feasible alternative but to float in the turbulence of the 1970s and 1980s. The inflation disparities were too large, the real economies required too much adjustment, the deficits too difficult to contain in a Bretton Woods straitjacket, however accommodating its binding. But in the 1990s many of the great disparities have been considerably reduced. Surely, it is said, there is now no excuse for the oscillations of exchange rates; best to eliminate or mute them in some new Bretton Woods arrangement.[7] One may presume that the discipline of Bretton Woods will prevent any large disparities and 'disequilibria' from developing. It is hard to accept this argument in the light of the fact that the old Bretton Woods had no such effect.

Variability of Real Exchange Rates

One of the enduring complaints against floating exchange rates is that there is much more variation in exchange rates than under a fixed or Bretton Woods type of system. This is of course entirely understandable with respect to nominal exchange rates. In a 'fixed but adjustable' system nominal exchange rates will move on 'realignment', as it is called in the EMS. But such movements should be infrequent. Generally, the nominal exchange rate will be contained between the bands (2 per cent in the case of Bretton Woods and 4.5 per cent in the EMS).

The more interesting question is the variability of *real* exchange rates. What is the effect of floating on the variability of competitiveness as reflected in the relative price ratios? There are no experimental data. Evidence can be adduced only from the historical record before and after 1972. A first reading is clear. The amount of real exchange rate variability, measured in virtually any pair of currencies, increased substantially after 1972.[8] Thus it does not seem that flexible movements in nominal exchange rates adjust to offset differential movements in domestic price levels.

This increased variability is puzzling. There is no theoretical reason why this should be so. Several *ad hoc* answers can be unearthed and used to rationalise the result. First, it may be claimed that before 1972 the system had stored up, and papered over, massive inconsistencies which had to be resolved over the next few years. This might have some plausibility for the mid-1970s, but the variability continued through to the end of the 1980s. Secondly, there were the oil shocks of 1973 and 1979 and the great inflations that were associated with, though not caused by, these events. Massive adjustments were needed. This may be true. But one suspects that it is not the whole story. I am inclined to believe that one powerful explanation is the emergence and phenomenal growth of private international capital markets. From 1969, these markets burgeoned. And the development of technology, together with the gradual reduction of regulations, has made speculation and cover less expensive.

I do not think that these explanations are at all adequate. This variability remains a puzzle and a challenge to the profession. To avoid misunderstanding it is necessary to emphasise that variability as such is not a bad or a good thing. It has to be judged along with all the alternatives available.

MONETARY POLICY AND INTERNATIONAL CO-ORDINATION

Basic Ideas on Co-ordination

ONE OF GOD'S greatest gifts to mankind was the free price system. It enables the co-operation and co-ordination in production of the most complex products, such as my word processor. Countless people have co-operated to produce and market this machine. Those who have so conjoined will never see one another and probably do not even know of the others' existence. They may speak different languages, have different religions and mores. Yet they co-ordinate their efforts, not through the directives of some super manager, but through their free choice among the teeming options offered by the free-market system.

The efficacy of the price system in achieving co-ordination and productive co-operation is well documented. Compared with a Gosplan, it is a marvel of freedom and efficiency. It is now widely accepted, even envied and emulated, in Eastern bloc countries as the only effective way of organising societies and their economies. It is natural to inquire whether the free price mechanism, which has been so successful in organising individuals and businesses, could not be equally applied to nation states.

From the chapters above, it is easy to see that there *is* a similar form of co-ordination through the price system. First, there needs to be freedom to make trades across national borders. Any severe restraint on this freedom will inhibit international co-operation. Secondly, one has to ensure that the price system can work by maintaining a fairly stable price level. But that is nothing new since it is needed for internal purposes. No system can work efficiently if the unit

51

of account is constantly and substantially changing its value. But different countries will have different views about what is the appropriate or tolerable rate of inflation. For example, Germany would regard a steady underlying inflation rate of 4 per cent as quite beyond the pale; whereas I suspect that most Americans would be content with such an inflation. Nevertheless, the citizens of Germany and the United States can happily co-ordinate with a zero inflation in Germany and 4 per cent in the United States, provided that no-one succeeds in fixing the dollar-mark exchange rate. Like any other price, the price of a mark in terms of dollars will adjust to the differential inflation rates.

Spillovers and Incentives

In this free price system there is no need for any explicit co-ordination of government monetary and fiscal policies. True, there will be spillovers from one country to another. The flexible exchange rate is no *'cordon sanitaire'*. Any undue expansion of the money supply in the United States will have *some* effect on Germany. The additional demand in the United States wll suck in imports from Germany. To pay for them dollars will flow into the accounts of German exporters. This will increase demand and prices in Germany. Some of the inflationary pressure in the United States will have been exported.[1]

But the pressure in Germany will be modest compared with that in the United States. If the inflation is made in the United States, then its main effects will be felt there, not in Germany. Thus, if the United States with its 4 per cent inflation target does expand the money supply by an amount which will give it, say, 6 per cent inflation, then the United States government and the Fed will have by far the greatest incentive to bring money under control once more so that it is in line with its 4 per cent norm. Similarly, by far the main effect of any undue expansion by the Bundesbank will be on the German, rather than the American, rate of inflation. Spillovers will be the second order effects. Thus *co-*

ordination is achieved by each government pursuing its own interest of stabilising its own price level. If each of the monetary authorities of the world designed policies to keep its domestic inflation down to its (presumed low) target, policies would be co-ordinated automatically through the medium of exchange rate and price and wage movements, and capital flows.

Granted the veracity of this argument, however, many observers will complain of the slow speed of adjustment, of possible overshoots, of speculative bubbles that bedevil markets, and of course of all the externalities. Surely it should be possible to speed up the adjustment process, to avoid excess speculation and many of the other mistakes of the market? This is the normal version of the case for co-ordination, central monitoring, and even some central international direction.[2]

Reality vs. the Ideal in Co-ordination

The first point to note about this argument is that, *on its own assumptions* it is logically impeccable. Clearly, if Germany and the United States knew all the effects, both domestic and international, of their policies, they could get together and fashion a joint arrangement which was, in aggregate, superior to the sum of their individual efforts. This is a subspecies of a more general argument used by utopians, socialists, and many schools of economists: *with perfect knowledge and foresight and unlimited powers of control, one can always improve on the free market.* Externalities, social costs and all those aspects which the market ignores or distorts can be taken into account by a benign bureaucracy in regulating markets.

Most of us, however, are rather sceptical about the efficacy of benign bureaucrats in regulating markets. The rise of the Public Choice school has made us aware that civil servants and politicians are moved by their own aims and ambitions. But political temptations are only part, and I think the smaller part, of the story. The main reason is the limitation of knowledge. Economists know very little about

53

the myriad of interacting processes that comprise markets. (Perhaps I should add that although economists know virtually nothing, they know more than politicians.) Chapter 2 told the story. But everyone will know how often economists' predictions are confounded.[3] We are abysmally ignorant about the macro-economic processes and the dynamics of forces that determine the fate of national economies. Any joint co-ordination of national policies would be based on pretentions which are completely unwarranted. It is likely that they would do more harm than good.

Persuasion and Sanctions

But even if one believes that economists are very clever and much more knowledgeable than I suppose, it is still difficult to see how co-ordination will be achieved in practice. How will all the ships of state be kept in line? What sanctions can be imposed? Although one may think of various shots across the bow, such as refusal to support a currency, the imposition of trade restrictions, etc., even the mere threat of such shots would surely scatter if not scuttle the convoy of co-operators. Co-ordination must depend on multilateral undertakings, goodwill, a community of interests, good faith and the salutary effects of the good example — rather weak reeds on which to lean in order to counter the self-interest of a nation state. If a government believes that it is in its interest to pursue non-co-operative policies, it will.[4]

There is an argument that co-ordination does help all participants to pursue non-inflationary financial policies. Suppose that the governments really do want to maintain responsible monetary and fiscal policies. But they have difficulty in convincing important groups of the electorate. In a round-up of the usual suspects the trade unions would be first in the bag. Then these governments, with the best of motives, can confront the trade unions with the fact of the co-ordination agreement. The government would say that it finds it impossible to agree to some outrageous wage increase because this would be inconsistent with its treaty obligations. As a general proposition, there seems to be something in it. We are all used to embracing rules which bind us in difficult cases. This argument has been adduced as one of the reasons for membership of the ERM by both Mr Lawson and Mr Brittan. It may well be true, but I remain doubtful. From my own inquiries, I have not yet found any wage negotiations that even considered, however remotely, the transitory variability of the exchange rate as one of the factors to be taken into account. Even corporations which have profits that much depend on the exchange rate appear to cover their commitments, for the year or so covering the wage contract. I believe it is up to the protagonists of the Lawson/Brittan view to offer some evidence for scrutiny if we are to credit their point of view with any substance.

On the international, as distinct from the European, co-ordination of economic policies generally, governments have paid considerable heed to the interest groups that command critical votes. Governments have not used the international agreement to confront such groups with the spectre of a government bound by 'foreign entanglements'. As the Americans say, 'it would not play in Peoria'. A short review of international co-ordination in the 1980s will help put British policies in their international context.

International Co-ordination in the 1980s

Perhaps the first substantial co-ordination of economic policies took place in the Bonn summit of 1978. From 1976 the Carter administration had embarked on a massive expansion, and by 1978 the inflation had risen to 9 per cent with obvious signs of much more to come.[5] Over the year the dollar had depreciated by about 15 per cent against the D-mark. At the summit the United States undertook to adopt more responsible policies (indeed, it argued that they were already largely in place), and in return Helmut Schmidt agreed that Germany would adopt more expansive measures, particularly in fiscal policy. For the German economy, this proved disastrous. There was already the beginnings of a massive German boom; the summit measures added fuel to the flames. Germany embarked on her own inflation from which she only slowly, and painfully, recovered in the early 1980s. Not the most auspicious beginning of post-Bretton Woods co-operation!

With the advent of Mrs Thatcher, Mr Reagan and Herr Kohl, international co-ordination became a secondary concern to the need to reduce inflation. Monetary control was the centrepiece of policy. Exchange rates were largely left to market forces, although they were occasionally used to corroborate whether monetary policy was suitably tight or too loose. Most of the summit countries reduced their fiscal deficits. The glaring exception was the United States. For reasons which are still the subject of much controversy, the Federal Government deficit rose in 1983 to about 6 per cent of GNP.

Virtually all the summits of the mid-1980s, even the late 1980s, were variations on the original sin of the US federal deficit. European and Japanese governments and central bankers have claimed that the federal deficit was responsible for high real interest rates, the high deficits on the current account of the US balance of payments (and their own unwanted surpluses), and for the 40 per cent real appreciation of the dollar to 1985. The high dollar in turn fuelled the protectionist movement in the United States, and undoubtedly frightened her trading partners.

There is little doubt that the soaring dollar, and the effects on both agriculture and the 'rust-belt' industries, wrought a profound change in the United States policy on exchange rates. It threatened the vote — or perhaps the vote threatened. In any case, Mr Baker, the new treasury secretary, thought that exchange rates should be managed to bring the dollar back to levels which he regarded as economically and politically acceptable.

Plaza and Louvre

The means by which the dollar was to be brought down, one would have thought, should have included the *bête noire* of the Europeans and Japanese — the federal deficit. Apart from the usual noises, however, Mr Baker entered no undertaking to increase taxes or reduce spending. In September 1985, the meeting at the Plaza (an hotel in New York) agreed that the main instrument would be co-ordinated intervention by the five central banks, but mainly by the Fed and the central banks of Germany and Japan. All three would sell their stocks of dollars for marks, yen, even for sterling and francs.

The fall of the dollar was sharp and sustained. The participants of the Plaza agreement have proclaimed the success of concerted intervention. Examination of the evidence, however, reveals that the fall of the dollar began in February 1985, some seven months *before* the start of implementation of the Plaza agreement. Inspection of the graph (see Figure 2) reveals that the dollar fell at roughly the same rate in the six months before the Plaza agreement as in the six months after it. It would appear that Plaza had no discernible effect.[6] But this in no way inhibited the participants from admiring their own perspicacity.

The fall of the dollar continued apace. By the end of 1986, fears of an undervalued dollar were rife. Overshooting and the inflationary consequences for the United States were the main impetus behind the Louvre agreement among the Group of Seven (G7)[7] countries in February 1987. By concerted intervention, Louvre aimed at supporting the dollar where it was, on the presumption that the rates were just right. The market, however, demurred. It anticipated a further decline. So the world's investors held off buying dollar bonds. Accepting their Louvre obligations, the central banks of Germany and Japan bought the excess offerings of dollar paper to an amount of more than $140 billion in 1987.

The Louvre agreement failed, in spite of sharp increases in US interest rates in mid-1987, contributing to the Wall Street crash of 19 October. In the next 10 weeks the dollar fell by 7

Figure 2:
The US Real Effective Exchange Rate, 1980-89
(Index: March 1973 = 100)

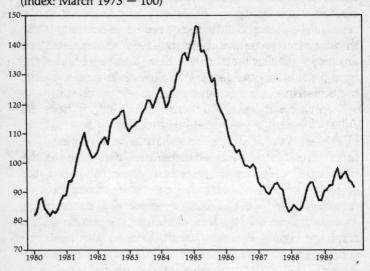

Note: Data are monthly.
Source: *Economic Report of the President*, February 1990; Board of Governors of the Federal Reserve System.

per cent against the G7 currencies (except the Canadian dollar). There had been a considerable expansion of marks, yen and even sterling in order to prop up the sinking dollar. The effects of these monetary expansions have produced many fears of inflation igniting again — and indeed we have seen that insidious upward pressure on prices in 1989, with perhaps some more to come in 1990.

In many respects the mid-1980s have been reminiscent of the other periods, 1969-72 and 1976-78, when there was massive intervention, more or less co-ordinated, by the attempts by central banks to manage exchange rates. Both ushered in a monetary expansion which culminated in the two deepest recessions of the post-war years. In the 1985-87 period, however, the world was saved from any substantial excess mainly by the most responsible behaviour of the Federal Reserve Board. (In particular, the courageous behaviour of the Fed's chairman, Alan Greenspan, must be given great credit for quashing the inflationary policy of his predecessor.) The speedy dethroning of exchange rate targets and the low monetary growth from mid-1987 onwards are good grounds for believing (in 1990) that the United States will have a stable and low rate of inflation over the early years of the decade.

Alternative Policies of Co-ordination:
(1) McKinnon

In the Plaza and Louvre initiatives, there was, so far as one can judge, no systematic theory on which the policy was based. Policy was guided largely by domestic political considerations. The US Treasury Secretary, James Baker, was reacting to the howls of rage from the 'rust' and farm belts. Economists, however, have developed theories which support specific policy *rules* for international co-ordination. Perhaps the most persuasive model is that of Ronald McKinnon.[8] McKinnon's basic argument is that in the modern world there are so many low-cost opportunities for people to switch between the major currencies (the dollar, Deutschemark and yen) that policies which pay sole concern to domestic money supplies are likely to produce serious disturbances and misalignments.

McKinnon suggests that we fix the exchange rates of the major currencies at roughly speaking PPP. Then the three countries should agree to a constant expansion rate for the *joint* money supply of all countries combined. The base case is when the three money supplies expand at the same rate (say, 4 per cent). But suppose that portfolio holders lose their taste for dollars and wish to acquire Deutschemarks? Then, according to McKinnon, the authorities should simply accommodate that currency substitution at the prevailing exchange rates. The Bundesbank would expand faster and the Fed would correspondingly reduce its monetary growth rate.

59

There is much to be said for this suggestion. But there is a fatal flaw. It offsets any transitory pressure on exchange rates brought about by changes in the demand for one currency in terms of another. This is not, however, the only cause of exchange rate strain. Many other real factors also affect market exchange rates. How can one identify simple portfolio shifts from these other real factors? I confess I do not know, even after the event, let alone contemporaneously, what was the true cause of the exchange rate pressure. And we know that in response to real factors, exchange rate adjustments are often the best way to adjust. Nevertheless, if the authorities do want a system of fixed exchange rates, some policy similar to McKinnon's must be the starting point for it. I suspect that the most likely result would not be fixed exchange rates but again a system of pseudo-fixity, and perhaps a decided inflationary bias similar to that which saw the end of Bretton Woods.

Alternative Policies of Co-ordination:
(2) Williamson's Target Zones

John Williamson has attempted to avoid many of the problems of rigidity in exchange rates in the Bretton Woods and McKinnon schemes.[9] First, instead of the 2 per cent band of Bretton Woods, he proposes a much broader band — perhaps as much as 20 per cent — within which the exchange rate could move without raising the issue of mandatory intervention. Secondly, the target zone should be given 'soft buffers' so that, if some unexpected shock threatened to push the rate out of the target zone, 'the authorities would cease defending the zone'. Thirdly, the zone would be used as a 'crawling' peg; this means that if the exchange rate were bumping against the lower bound for some (specified?) time, the whole target zone would be moved downwards by a predetermined amount. Fourthly, there would be regular 'reviews' of the real exchange rate target. Lastly, monetary and fiscal policy would be adjusted to avoid major interventions.

It is difficult to claim that the Williamson system lacks

flexibility. Indeed, suitably interpreted, it seems little different from a free float. But it *is* different. It invokes intervention and 'reviews' when any large exchange rate movement takes place. It would, for example, have induced intervention and reviews of the Deutschemark in 1977-78, of sterling in 1979-81, and of the dollar in 1981-85. What such intervention and reviews would have accomplished is, of course, another matter. Would they, for example, have undermined the anti-inflationary squeeze of the early 1980s in the United States and Britain? We do not know the answer, but it can be said with certainty that the Williamson framework would have had some effect in modifying the disinflationary policy.

There is so much room for interpretation and dissension in the target zone proposals that it is difficult to see it as an appropriate basis for any agreed system of co-ordination. Financial commentators, such as Hobart Rowan and Samuel Brittan, have lavished their approval on the target zone proposals.[10] It was reported that the proposals, in some form or other, were widely accepted as the way forward. After the collapse of the Louvre agreement, however, the proposals seem to have lost some of their glitter. I suspect that this is in part due to the recognition that we do *not* know much at all about the so-called fundamental equilibrium real exchange rate. Experts disagree on the concept and the measures.

In my view, if the target zone is effective, it will give rise to massive speculative capital movements which are such a bane to any pseudo-fixed rate system. Perhaps the signals of impending devaluation are more blurred than under Bretton Woods. But a complete obfuscation of signals would be similar to flexible rates. Thus if it is effective it is bad, and if it is ineffective it is otiose.

Appropriate Co-ordination

Is there *any* role for co-ordination? Looking at the performance of co-ordination during the last decade or so would give one pause. Herb Stein has characterised most of the co-ordination recently as each country telling other countries how they should conduct their economic policy. Nevertheless, I think there is a case for co-ordination. But it should have modest goals and a minimum of mandatory measures and sanctions. Clearly, it is a good idea for ministers of finance to keep each other informed of their views about domestic policies, and, indeed, their views about each other's economic policy. There is a role for friendly discussion and persuasion. But there is also a great need for tolerance. Each country will have different ideas about the best way forward. None is the custodian of the 'correct' model. Humble pie should be the daily diet of ministers and their advisers.

There is room for deals to be made, provided they are in the mutual interests of the parties and do not involve any binding commitments on future governments, or discrimination against any excluded party. Meetings of the G7 or 'summits' are not the appropriate place for ministers to play political games in pursuit of maximising strategies. Similarly, they are not the occasions, as have occurred frequently in the last eight years, for grandstanding accusations of one government by the others. Quiet informed exchange of facts and opinions is the best way forward.[11]

MONETARY SYSTEMS
FOR EUROPE

Antecedents — The EPU and Sterling Area

SINCE THE SECOND WORLD WAR various forms of monetary co-operation have appeared in Europe. The first effective one was the European Payments Union (EPU). This was fashioned in response to the dollar shortage in the 1940s and 1950s. In the framework of Bretton Woods, it enabled the members of the EPU to have limited convertibility with one another while discriminating against the dollar (using the scarce currency clause of the Bretton Woods agreement) in their exchange controls. The EPU undoubtedly introduced a degree of multilateral clearing and trade. It was a great improvement on the bilateral deals of the inter-war years. By the end of the 1950s, however, the dollar shortage was largely over — at least for the major European countries. Full external convertibility became the norm for Germany, France and the UK as well as for the many other smaller European countries. The EPU, therefore, became redundant.

There were other attempts to have convertible currencies within blocs. In the aftermath of the Second World War, Britain ran such a system in the sterling area. Some countries, generally members of the Commonwealth or Empire, based their currency on sterling. The currency board system was the model for such arrangements. Such boards held sterling to exchange at the fixed rate for the colonial or commonwealth currency. In practice, much of the reserve was held on deposit in London. The sterling area worked quite well for some years. But it fell apart in the mid-1960s. Sterling was obviously precarious and therefore in no position to remain a reserve currency. The devaluation of sterling in 1967 put the finishing touches to its corpse.

The 'Snake'

The breakdown of Bretton Woods was soon followed by attempts to resuscitate it, in the Smithsonian agreement of January 1972. It soon failed. Concurrently, the idea of monetary union in the EEC, mainly the brainchild of Raymond Barre, had been incorporated in the Werner Report of 1970. The basic proposal was to reduce currency fluctuations in Europe and to establish a machinery to 'co-ordinate' economic policies. In the early months of 1972 the European countries entered into an agreement to keep their currencies in line with one another, floating as a group against the dollar. The four major currencies — Deutschemark, sterling, franc and lira — were joined by a number of minor currencies in forming the 'snake'. Each country had the responsibility of keeping its currency in line with the others and there were understandings, but no undertakings, that there would be assistance forthcoming in time of need. There was no arrangement to co-ordinate financial policies, as Barre had urged in the Werner Report. In the view of many observers, this was a fatal flaw.

Unfortunately, the snake soon slid into the crises that beset all countries from 1973. The snake could not digest the rapid and variable rates of inflation together with the large capital movements. Three of the major currencies — sterling, franc and lira — defected, leaving only the Deutschemark and its satellite currencies. The snake became very bloated and permissive with few pretentions to being a fixed-rate system.

The EMS and the ERM[1]

The creators of the European Monetary System in 1978 were Chancellor Helmut Schmidt and President Giscard d'Estaing. The motives for joining have been much discussed. It has been argued, for example by Samuel Brittan, that Helmut Schmidt was simply searching for a way of dealing with the flight from the Carter dollar into the mark and wanted a convenient way of diffusing the inflow to his European partners. I suspect that President Giscard d'Estaing saw it as an opportunity to link France more closely to the mighty German economy, and at the same time he believed that it would give some French control over the tide of German monetary policy. And it was a step on the way to a world of managed exchange rates — a consistent theme of much French policy. Possibly it was seen as a way of reviving the ideal of a united Europe — a much tarnished ideal in the Europe of the late 1970s. It is also interesting to note that, at inception, the independent Bundesbank was against it, probably because of the unhappy experience with defending parities in the 1970s. Gradually the Bundesbank became 'cautiously positive'.[2] Many of the smaller countries, such as Eire, went along with the EMS idea because they conceived it as a form of help from the mighty German economy. And to the Netherlands, it meant little change from their existing fix.

Whatever the motives, the leaders and their expert advisers had noted the problems with the snake, and believed that these could be solved by creating mandatory help with intervention. This arrangement — exchange rates contained in a band and mandatory assistance — comprises the Exchange Rate Mechanism (ERM). Thus a member under exchange rate pressure could rely on short-term support from other members. All the countries of the EEC are members of the EMS and are *entitled* to join the ERM. But they are *not required* to join the ERM. Thus Britain, Greece and Portugal are members of the EMS but do not participate in the ERM. In common parlance it is said that these countries have not joined the EMS. Although not strictly correct, this usage is so widespread that I will occasionally use it in this book.

In principle, a weak currency country can have access to automatic and, again in principle, unlimited credit through

65

Table 1:
Exchange Rate Realignments Within the EMS, 1979-87

		DM	HFL	FF	BFR	LIT	DKR	IRISH £
24 Sept.	1979	2.0	—	—	—	—	−2.9	—
30 Nov.	1979	—	—	—	—	—	−4.8	—
23 Mar.	1981	—	—	—	—	−6.0	—	—
5 Oct.	1981	5.5	5.5	−3.0	—	−3.0	—	—
22 Feb.	1982	—	—	—	−8.5	—	−3.0	—
14 Jun.	1982	4.25	4.25	−5.75	—	−2.75	—	—
21 Mar.	1983	5.5	3.5	−2.5	1.5	−2.5	2.5	−3.5
22 Jul.	1985	2.0	2.0	2.0	2.0	−6.0	2.0	2.0
7 Apr.	1986	3.0	3.0	−3.0	1.0	—	1.0	—
4 Aug.	1986	—	—	—	—	—	—	−8.0
12 Jan.	1987	3.0	3.0	—	2.0	—	—	—

Notes: (1) The numbers are percentage changes of a given currency's bilateral central rate against those currencies whose bilateral parities were not realigned. A positive number denotes an appreciation, and a negative number denotes a depreciation. On 21 March 1983, and on 22 July 1986, all parities were realigned. BFR — Belgium/Luxembourg franc, DKR — Danish kroner, DM — Deutschemark, FF — French franc, LIT — Italian lira, IRISH £ — Irish pound, HFL — Netherlands guilder.

(2) The Italian lira was devalued by about 3.7% with respect to its central rate on 8 January 1990. But since the band was narrowed from 6% to 2.25%, the lower limit remained the same.

Source: Dorn and Niskanen (eds.), *op. cit.,* page 277; Commission of the European Communities.

the Very Short-Term Financing Facility.[3] This mutual support system has varied over the life of the ERM. And different countries have given it different interpretations at different times. There have been numerous complaints, however, about the mechanism of central bank intervention in the foreign exchange markets. In particular, Germany has felt the weight of the burden of support.[4]

The Band and Realignments

The normal requirement of the ERM is to maintain the exchange rate around the central value plus or minus 2.25 per cent. Italy (until January 1990) and Spain, however, have

Table 2:
EMS/ERM Countries: Percentage Change in Bilateral Parities from 13 March 1979 to 12 January 1987

	BFR	DKR	DM	FF	LIT	IRISH £	HFL
BFR		2.94	−27.18	10.13	18.30	7.48	−23.29
DKR			−30.12	7.19	14.75	4.54	−26.23
DM				37.31	45.48	34.16	3.89
FF					8.18	−2.64	−34.81
LIT						−10.82	−41.59
IRISH £							−30.77

Note: A positive number denotes a devaluation, and a minus sign denotes an appreciation of the currency shown in the column heading with respect to the currency shown in the row heading.

Sources: H. Ungener, O. Evans, T. Mayer and P. Young, *The European Monetary System: Recent Developments*, IMF Occasional Paper 48, Washington DC: IMF, 1986, Table 6; and San Paolo, *ECU Newsletter*, January 1987.

elected to maintain their exchange rates within a plus or minus 6 per cent band. Within these constraints, however, countries have pursued more restrictive policies. Thus the Netherlands, so closely tied in to the West German economy, has virtually locked itself to the Deutschemark. Other countries outside the EMS and ERM, but closely integrated with the German economy, have also pegged their currencies with some rigidity to the German mark: the most notable example is Austria. And it is generally true that members try to avoid straying near the limits of toleration. Rarely does a member allow its currency to bump along at the lower level of the band.

The EMS allows for the 'realignment' of currencies at new central parities. In the 10 years from 1979 to 1989, there have been 11 parity changes (see Table 1). These realignments were much more frequent in the early days when there was a need to adjust to very diffferent rates of inflation. Since January 1987 there has been only one adjustment of the central values, the devaluation of the lira in January 1990 as it entered the 2.25 per cent band. But it is widely thought

67

that the disparities have become so large that a substantial realignment cannot be long delayed.

The process of realignment was meant to proceed from a deliberation on the fundamentals, particularly relative growth and inflation rates. In practice the currencies have often been pushed, often precipitously, into a realignment in order to counter speculative capital movements. The market has a number of signals it can read to see when a realignment is imminent. Ministers and central bankers become agitated and leaks soon spring forth. This provides a rich nectar for the busy bees of private speculation.

Aims of the EMS/ERM

The EMS was created to achieve 'a zone of monetary stability in Europe' that would eventually develop into a European Monetary Fund. What is meant by monetary stability? Certainly the basic idea was exchange rate stability. But that can be interpreted in various ways. The first is that the EMS would reduce the day-to-day or weekly and monthly variations in exchange rates. (Much of the casual criticism of the floating system by traders and vacationers was in terms of the difficulty of planning short-term operations.) The second is that there would be more long-term stability in exchange rates. (See Table 2 for the cumulative changes in ERM countries.) That is to say, the exchange rates would not sink or rise consistently, year in year out. The corollary is that there would be little divergence in rates of inflation — this is the so-called 'convergence' objective.

There is little doubt about which is the most important goal. It is useful to reduce the variability of exchange rates, provided that one does not thereby introduce even more damaging distortions elsewhere. But, for the majority of transactions, it is always possible to buy cover in the thick forward market for short periods ahead. On the other hand, it is impossible to buy any cover for inflation losses (with the rather limited exception of indexed gilts). The long-term stability of exchange rates, provided it is not behind a barrier of controls, is clearly the most important objective. But it needs to be interpreted in a subtle way. The underlying objective is, of course, stability of prices or, at least, stability of low (*circa* 2 per cent) inflation. Then to achieve, say, zero inflation in the long run may require a long-term appreciation against the dollar or even against the European Currency Unit (ECU) (a basket of European currencies) or against Special Drawing Rights (SDRs) (a basket of the five most important currencies). In short, if the world or Europe or even Germany goes on an inflationary (or deflationary) binge, long-term stability of the exchange rate is a recipe for importing such price movements.

The EMS and German Hegemony

This discussion highlights a central issue: Who actually runs the EMS/ERM? Like most multinational institutions, the EMS was set up formally as an institution with equal participation by all members.[5] National prides demand no less. In a democratic institution all nations were to be equal. The reality, however, was quite different. Some were more equal than others. In the event Germany became the price leader and in effect dominated policy. This German hegemony has been much resented by France and Italy, among others. Because of their reluctance to realign, French financial policy is largely determined by the Bundesbank, over which the government of France has virtually no control and little influence. Indeed, because of the statutory independence of the Bundesbank, the German government has only influence, not power, to affect monetary policy – so even if France brought pressure to bear on the German government, such pressure would be much dissipated by the time it found its way from Bonn to Frankfurt. The Bundesbank ruled.[6]

This should have surprised no-one. Germany was the biggest and richest economy with the most liberal markets in continental Europe. The German reserves were unmatched, and, corresponding to its role as a major exporter of goods, Germany had become an important exporter of capital.

69

Above all, the Deutschemark was rightly seen as the most inflation-free of all the major currencies (including the dollar).

The Bundesbank enjoyed credibility as the guardian of monetary propriety. The other countries believed that by joining the ERM they would also acquire credibility for their currencies and credibility for their policies. But this would be possible only if the Bundesbank were seen to be in a position to maintain its responsible policies. And it was widely accepted that the Bundesbank's independence, as well as the abiding fear of inflation in Germany, was a critical element of that credibility.

Here was a central dilemma. In order to have more 'democratic' control of the EMS policy (what the French call 'symmetry'), it is necessary to allow the French, Italians, and others due influence in formulating German monetary policy. But such influence would clearly erode and eventually destroy the independence of the Bundesbank on which the whole edifice of credibility is built.[7] Thus if the EMS is to achieve its major function, it must be dominated by the élite and unelected Bundesbank, and democracy be damned! Inevitably, such a concentration of power has caused much tension. For example, in January 1987, because France differed so much with the Bundesbank's restrictive policy, France refused to intervene when the franc fell to the floor. In the event the Bundesbank, fearful of wrecking the ERM, bought francs to put it back in the fold. The resentment of German power and influence is a worrying resuscitation of an old theme of European politics.

As we shall see, this fundamental dilemma is inherent in any system similar to the EMS. And it gives rise to similar types of political tensions. There is little to be done that would resolve the inconsistencies of objectives. One ideal way would be for France, Italy, and others to acquire, in their own right, a credibility as convincing as that of the Bundesbank. Not only is this idle speculation, but then, of course, there would be no need for an EMS to achieve the convergence of inflation rates. There would then be a possibility for more non-German participation in policy. But still the union would be dominated by Germany. This has led some commentators, among whom one must number several Presidents of France, to suggest that the only way to solve the problem of German monetary hegemony is a return to a gold standard. But later I shall suggest other solutions.

It may appear that, as the leader of the EMS, Germany has substantial freedom to pursue its own monetary and fiscal policy. It looks like Deutschland uber alles — or at least alles participants in the ERM. But, paradoxically, Germany is also a prisoner of the ERM. Because of the reluctance to realign, Germany is prevented from pursuing a monetary policy that the Bundesbank believes is consistent with its obligation to avoid inflation. Just as in the late 1960s and to August 1971, the United States complained that, as the anchor of the Bretton Woods system, it alone could not devalue the dollar against the mark, so, as the linchpin of the EMS, Germany cannot unilaterally revalue the mark against its main trading partners in the ERM. The Bundesbank has some apparent freedom to raise interest rates, but pressure to prevent such a rise from France and Italy is as likely to be as intense as the resistance to realignment. Germany is hardly the dog that wags the ERM tail. As Karl Otto Pöhl must know, it is the tail that dogs the wag.

The Performance of the EMS: Exchange Rates[8]

It is extraordinarily difficult to make assessments of the performance of the EMS that command everyone's confidence. The normal method of judging the EMS is to pursue two sorts of comparisons. First, one may compare what happened to participants before 1979 and after — a time-series approach. Secondly, from 1979 a comparison may be made between those countries involved in the ERM and those which stayed aloof — a cross-section approach. The time-series approach has the advantage that one can

71

compare the same country, with all its many constant individual characteristics, before and after. But of course countries would have changed their performance in the absence of the EMS, and consequently we do not know how much of the change to attribute to ERM membership. The cross-section comparisons suffer from the fact that countries will vary considerably in performance, and participation in the ERM will be one factor among many others. Nevertheless, these two approaches do give some basis for judging performance. A third — the modelling approach — has been tried by Patrick Minford. In order to produce a standard for comparison, he models what would have happened in the absence of ERM membership, thus giving a 'counterfactual' account against which to compare the real record.

One quite remarkable result of these empirical inquiries is that they all tell broadly the same story. First, let us look at exchange rate variability. The most obvious point is that *bilateral* exchange rate variability between ERM participants is less than in the years before 1979. This was one of the aims of the EMS and it has been achieved. This does not mean, however, that there has been any gain in stability of *effective* exchange rates or that exchange rate variability with other OECD countries has not increased. Indeed, the second result confirms that whatever stability had been achieved in bilateral rates was more than offset by increases in variability with respect to non-ERM currencies.

In short, the ERM provided some intra-ERM stability which was *more than offset* by increased external variability. And this result carries over to *real* exchange rates. Thus the increased external variability in nominal rates was not fully offset by differential rates of inflation. All these conclusions held whether one compared experience before 1979 with that after, or whether one analysed the ERM countries compared with those outside.[9]

The Performance of the EMS: Inflation, Trade and Growth[10]

But one of the abiding claims for the EMS is as a discipline on inflation: the participants acquire the credibility of the Bundesbank. Perhaps so, but it is not evident from the statistics.

In the ERM countries, the (weighted) average rate of inflation decreased more slowly than in the rest of the OECD countries. Even confining the discussion to Europe, the decline in the ERM countries was less than that in other OECD European countries. Furthermore, the inflation rate in the ERM was, in 1986, rather higher than that in the other OECD countries. From 1987 on, these relationships become blurred by sterling's shadowing of the mark and, in aggregate, by the various interventions and monetary policies induced by the Louvre and other 'agreements'.

What about the variability of inflation? Contrary to assertions frequently made by the pro-EMS lobby, convergence on inflation took *longer* in the EMS than in the rest of the OECD. Furthermore, over the life of the ERM (to 1986) the dispersion of inflation rates has been much larger in the ERM countries than among the major OECD countries. Indeed, comparing the seven years before with the seven years after 1979, among ERM countries the dispersion of inflation rates *increased*, whereas in the other OECD countries the dispersion fell.

The stability of nominal bilateral exchange rates should, according to the EMS's apologists, promote trade by reducing the exchange risk. The growth of trade within the ERM, however, compares most unfavourably with the growth of trade with non-EMS countries.[11] The (unweighted) average of the five old EMS members' growth of trade with one another from 1979 to 1984 was 0.6 per cent compared with 4.1 per cent with non-ERM countries.

Finally, growth of real investment and GDP was much slower in the ERM countries than in the other OECD countries (see Table 3). After 1979, growth and investment

Table 3:
Macro-economic Performance of EMS and Non-EMS
Industrialised Countries, 1973-78 and 1979-85

(per cent per annum)

	EMS	Non-EMS	European Non-EMS
Growth of GDP (yearly average)			
1973-78:	2.8	2.9	1.9
1979-85:	1.7	2.7	1.8
Growth of Investment (yearly average)			
1973-78:	1.4	2.8	−0.2
1979-85:	0.3	2.5	0.4
Inflation rate (yearly average)			
1973-78:	9.1	9.6	12.5
1979-85:	8.3	6.9	8.8
1985:	4.8	3.8	5.9

Notes: (1) The *Non-EMS countries* are the following: Austria, Norway, Sweden, Switzerland, Finland, Spain, UK, Canada, US, Japan. The *European Non-EMS* consists of the same countries excluding the US, Japan and Canada.

(2) The averages of each group of countries are obtained using GDP weights.

Source: OECD, Main Economic Indicators.

declined more than in the other OECD countries. And in European non-EMS countries, investment growth actually increased.

The EMS — Modelled Results

All these conclusions are from the actual historical record. And they are properly subject to the argument that we do not know what would have happened in the absence of the EMS in the years following 1979. It might be suggested that, if the EMS had not been created, the performance of the ERM countries would have been much worse. Although there is no irrefutable way of dealing with such an allegation,

Patrick Minford has performed a great service by modelling the EMS in its world context.[12] The results are complex but clear. As Minford puts it:

> '... the EMS system gives somewhat poorer overall stability than floating to the "dependent-currency" participating countries — that is France, Italy and the UK ... the reason ... is that the EMS, with its deflationary bias for the dependent-currency countries, causes them to over-react in a deflationary direction to the shock [of 4 per cent increase in monetary growth for two years].'

In the absence of the EMS, the (shock) increase in monetary growth would be associated with a fall in both the nominal *and the real* exchange rate. There is a rise in the rate of inflation, but demand increases and output and net exports also go up. In the EMS, the constraint on the movement of the exchange rate means that price and wage increases cause an *appreciation* of the real exchange rate. Thus the dependent countries suffer from the reduction in net export demand due to the real appreciation and from an increase in inflation. These are, of course, the transitory effects. Ultimately, the dependent country must either devalue (realign) or deflate, in order to counter the effects of the original monetary expansion.

Minford's model does seem not to conflict with the descriptions by Vaubel, Fratianni, etc. The EMS induces a perverse appreciation of the real exchange rate, and this leads to unnecessary output losses in adjusting to the monetary shock. On the other hand, countries that are not Bundesbank dependent gain somewhat from the over-valuation of the French franc, the Italian lira, etc. The obvious example is Germany, but also the United States and Japan are able to secure some of the markets of France, Italy, and so on.

EMS adherents will, of course, argue that these model runs are not really relevant, since the EMS will be more likely to *prevent* a monetary shock than if one is outside the ERM. Such an allegation requires more than assertion to give it credibility, especially in view of the behaviour of the United Kingdom during the shadowing of the Deutschemark in 1987-88. Indeed, on that occasion 'joining' the ERM club actually *caused* the monetary explosion.

The EMS and Persistence of Overvaluation

Granted that there is more inertial inflationary pressure in France and Italy, it is possible that this Minford mechanism explains some part of the chronic overvaluation of the franc and the lira. And this overvaluation has occurred in spite of the use of exchange controls, on occasion most restrictive controls, during the life of the EMS. It is never easy, however, to demonstrate that an exchange rate is above the value that would emerge in a free market, but the persistence of the large German current balance-of-payments surpluses in relation to its fellow-EMS participants does suggest that the overvaluation has been chronic and substantial.

I suspect that the reason must be sought in the lore of politics. There is no doubt that, politically, realignment, however justified, is viewed as a policy failure. The long reluctance of politicians to concede to a devaluation contributes to chronic overvaluation of the dependent currencies. But there is the additional question: Why is it that, when they do devalue, the devaluation is such that the currency is just about brought into line with its deteriorated purchasing power? Why do they not devalue sufficiently so that, on the average up to the time of the next realignment, the currency is not persistently overvalued? If, for example, one examines sterling's devaluation in 1949, most authorities were clear that in PPP terms it was overdone (from $4.20 to $2.80). Sterling was then undervalued for some years. At the time it was thought that this was an appropriate policy, since one had to ensure that the markets would not expect another devaluation to follow for many years. So it turned out.

In the case of the EMS, however, one suspects that the reason for the reluctance of ERM members to devalue sufficiently is that the central banks believe, rightly or wrongly, that such devaluations would signal a country's choice of a lax policy on inflation. The country would be thought to be not merely making up for past laxity but also preparing for new monetary expansions. If this is so, the persistent overvaluation of the currency is a high price to pay for such a reputation and credibility.

Germany and Credibility

One of the oft-repeated arguments for ERM membership is the 'credibility' argument — members latch on to the stability of the Bundesbank. The view that by hanging on to the coat-tails of the Bundesbank, members reduced the costs of disinflation has been discredited by the data. Countries outside the ERM did rather better. But we must ask the additional question: What does Germany gain from being in the ERM?

Initially the Bundesbank strongly opposed the EMS. In one of the rare capitulations of the Bundesbank to political pressure, Helmut Schmidt foisted it on them. There is no doubt that Schmidt saw considerable political gains to be garnered from polishing up a very tarnished image of the Common Market. The relaunch of European integration was one of the achievements of both Schmidt and Giscard d'Estaing. The creation of a free-trade area and the removal of controls on capital and labour flows could, of course, have gone ahead, I believe rather more easily, without the apparatus of the EMS. But it was an important political symbol. As the Bundesbank surmised, however, the economic benefits to Germany were, and remain, much less clear.

The Bundesbank's responsibility was defined in its constitution as the defence of the domestic value of the mark. It had never relished the role of the mark as a reserve currency. The demands on the mark as a reserve currency may often be inconsistent with the policy of domestic stability. But the emergence of the mark as one of the three great currencies meant that it could not avoid some of the problems of being, for example, one of the main custodians of speculative flows out of the dollar. In such circumstances, the EMS might be seen as a way of diffusing those flows to other members. However, the other members of the EMS (except the Netherlands) maintained not merely exchange controls but also a formidable battery of other credit and capital regulations which were designed, *inter alia*, to ward off such speculative flows. Ironically, it was the non-ERM member, the United Kingdom, with its wide open capital markets in the 1980s, which became, after Germany, the next most important recipient of speculative flows. If the price of the ERM was continued capital controls, then Germany was, on this score, a net loser.

The Bundesbank's behaviour with the EMS is almost certainly different from the policy it would have pursued in the absence of the EMS. The pseudo-fixed system ensures that, if Germany pursued an expansionary monetary policy, the inflationary costs would be more spread over the other members than if there was a floating-rate régime. Thus there would be less incentive for the Bundesbank to keep money tight, and more incentive to inflate.[13] This raises expectations of a higher average rate of inflation throughout the EMS. Not only does Germany not gain from her membership, but the credibility gain is more disputable.

In general, one may conclude that the fears expressed by the Bundesbank, and overridden by Helmut Schmidt, were well founded.[14]

A Fundamental, Even Fatal, Flaw in the EMS

In the old gold standard system, there were automatic mechanisms which, in response to some external event such as a physical calamity or to some internal 'error', would restore the equilibrium of the system. For example, the loss of a country's main grain crop would give rise to increased prices and net imports which would be financed in part by exports of gold. This would reduce the reserves and the money stock to bring the price level back into line with the rest of the world (where both gold reserves, money stock and prices would rise). It was a self-correcting system.[15]

There is no inherent self-correction in the EMS. On the contrary, in its pure form the system will provide perverse signals. In order to demonstrate such perversity, I fear that we must specify more precisely how an ideal EMS works. Of course, such an ideal will not include either exchange controls or, more importantly, those barriers and restrictions which are imposed on domestic institutions in order to prevent or inhibit the residents from choosing freely the denomination of their assets and debts. I shall therefore assume that, in this broad sense, there are no exchange controls. Since the objective of the EMS was to provide an 'area of stability', let us assume that the exchange rates between participants are actually *fixed for a specified period*, then realigned. The actual period during which they can be presumed fixed will vary according to the divergences in inflation rates — the smaller the diversion the longer the time between realignments.

Let us suppose that the period is one year.[16] If everyone knows that exchange rates are fixed for that year, then nominal interest rates on financial instruments which originate and mature in that year will be approximately the same for all participants in the ERM. Arbitrage will ensure this near equality. For if the rate of interest in Italy substantially exceeds that in Germany, it will pay all asset holders to switch to lira, that is, to borrow in Deutschemarks and invest in lira for that period of fixity of the lira-mark exchange rate. This is no more than the application of the 'law of one price' to financial instruments. (In this case, because of the fixed rate of exchange, the cost of forward cover for the transaction is zero.)

Thus the EMS forces countries to have the same nominal interest rates. If, however, Italy is inflating at a rate of 7 per cent and Germany at a rate of 2 per cent (both over the relevant period of fixity), then there is a problem of perversity. With the same interest rate at, say, 5 per cent, the

How is short r set?

real rate of interest for Italy is *minus* 2 per cent and for Germany *plus* 3 per cent. Thus Italy will have an expansionary monetary policy, while Germany will pursue one of restraint. But this will exacerbate inflation in Italy and yet restrain further the already low inflation in Germany. This is the opposite of 'convergence', namely, it induces divergence.

Realignment Dynamics

Such perverse forces cannot continue for long. As the date, assumed known and fixed, for realignment approaches, so the interest rates, for shorter and shorter maturities, will reflect the expected depreciation of the lira. It will pay speculators to borrow lira and buy mark financial assets to cash in on their appreciation at the realignment. This will cause lira interest rates on maturities that cover the realignment date to rise well above corresponding German rates; the difference will reflect the expected change in the exchange rate. When the maturity is overnight corresponding to the realignment, lira rates of interest may rise to hundreds of per cent. Of course, the interest rate differential is at last in the right direction; that is, the high inflation country has the high rates and the low inflation country the low ones.

It is unlikely, however, that these interest rates would be the pattern which would be chosen by a minister of finance who, unconstrained by membership of the ERM, was pursuing a disinflationary domestic policy. But, more importantly, after realignment and with Italy still inflating at 7 per cent and Germany at 2 per cent, the system reverts again to the *status quo ante*. With the exchange rates fixed for the next year, Italy and Germany will have the same interest rates and the same perverse effects on monetary growth.

This sort of effect can be observed in the Lawson decision to peg sterling to the mark at DM3.00 in early 1987. With British interest rates at about 5 per cent above those in Germany, a fixed exchange rate gave rise to a great influx of capital. This put considerable pressure on British interest rates and, in spite of the manifest inflationary pressure, they were brought down to 7.5 per cent. Although, as we shall see, the authorities allowed the mark-sterling rate to rise from March 1988, this was an overshoot before the inevitable high interest rates and devaluation (or 're-alignment').[17] The details of that story will be told in Chapter 6.

Uncertain Realignments and Moving in the Band

This model of the ERM is a caricature. It delineates, even exaggerates, the strengths and weaknesses of the pure EMS. But as a working institution the EMS is anything but pure. For example, the exchange rates can move within the band, so that in principle there can be a 4.5 per cent devaluation (or 12 per cent in the case of Spain). Participant countries, however, usually try to keep their rates somewhere in the immediate vicinity of the central rate, presumably because any bumping against the limits would signal the likelihood of a realignment.

This brings us to the assumptions we made in the model, namely, that the time of the realignment is known with certainty. This is not the case. Although they are not complete surprises, the realignments of various dimensions can be predicted only with large uncertainties attached. But it is usually quite easy to predict the *direction* of the realignment — the French franc and the lira will go down against the Deutschemark. Thus the shadow of devaluation is cast forward in time and increases interest rates in Italy relative to those in Germany. But again, whether that devaluation 'shadow effect' is consistent with what a prudential finance minister would require to cope with domestic conditions in Italy is another matter.

One may reflect that it is odd that it is the *uncertainty* of exchange rates in the ERM that makes it possible for Italy to pursue disinflationary monetary policies and for Germany to avoid inflationary ones. The EMS was to be an island of

81

stability and certainty in a sea of floating flotsam. But it is only the uncertainty that keeps it above water.

Exchange Controls and the Consequences of Freedom

Participants in the ERM can pursue deviant interest-rate policies if they are protected by suitably high controls. Behind the controls the authorities can increase interest rates, knowing that they can regulate the import of capital. Such exchange controls have been characteristic of France and Italy during the life of the EMS. They are required to be eliminated by mid-1990. Indeed, overt exchange controls have been substantially reduced over the years 1987-89. As one would expect, the Eurofranc and Eurolira market rates have more closely approached the rates of interest on domestic markets in France and Italy. And in January 1990, Italy embraced the 2.25 per cent band. All this suggests that the equality of nominal interest rates will become more of a reality of the ERM.

In 1990, it has been suggested by Messrs Francesco Giavazzi and Luigi Spaventa that since overt exchange controls have now been eliminated among the main participants of the ERM, governments cannot risk a realignment.[18] Any hint of a realignment will cause such speculative capital flows, untrammelled by controls, that governments will not be able to maintain domestic stability. It is conceded that there will be downward pressure on real interest rates in the inflating countries and that this will push up inflation in the short run. But it is argued that the appreciation of the *real* exchange rate, together with rigid *nominal* exchange rates, will so influence expectations that businessmen will become convinced that they cannot raise prices and that they must resist trade union pressure. Thus will inflation be conquered, convergence be complete and the old central rates maintained.

This argument may well be correct. It leans very heavily on expectations all accommodating to the fixed exchange rate. We know very little about expectations and they may behave in the manner the authors claim. One must have grave doubts, however, that any such adjustments occur. We have a long historical record — Britain in 1926-31 and in 1987-90, Chile in 1979-83, and many other examples — to show that too high a real exchange rate distorts the economy, raises the relative prices of domestic goods and depresses the prices of traded goods. It rarely defeats expectations of inflation. Furthermore, for Giavazzi and Spaventa's system of fixed parities to be validated, it must mean that over some period the inflationary countries must inflate at a rate *less than* that of Germany. For example, if Germany's inflation rate is 2 per cent and Italy has been inflating for, say, three years at 6 per cent, then to recover lost ground in the next three years, Italy must have a *deflation* of 2 per cent per annum for those years. Possible, perhaps, but hardly plausible.

Similarly, it appears that the Italian authorities, while conceding that the lira interest rate is constrained by the ERM to be negative in real terms and a powerful stimulus to demand and inflation, would be simultaneously intoning their absolute opposition to 'long-run' inflation as manifest in their determination to hold the nominal exchange rate. It is analogous to the drug addict who swears off drugs, but only after the next fix. I find it difficult to believe in such an inconsistent package of policies. It will be accepted only by the most credulous.

Messrs Giavazzi and Spaveta are really describing a knife-edge type of equilibrium. Let us assume, for example, that Italy and Germany have converged so that they have the same rate of inflation. Then they may comfortably have the same nominal and real interest rates. There is *de facto* union, and exchange rates can remain fixed. Everyone may well be convinced that they will remain so and expectations will be validated. The ERM will be required to cope with incidental increases in the demand for money by one country and the reduction in demand by another country, by maintaining the same interest rates. But this state of perfection is hardly of interest. We know that we cannot identify all the trials and tribulations and offset them to produce such a model of stability. What we need is a system that will deal with perturbations and shocks, such as monetary mistakes and natural disasters. Suppose, for example, that someone makes a mistake and there is an accidental increase in the Italian rate of inflation. Then, alas, we will have all the inconsistencies and perversities that are discussed above.

Is the 'Walters Critique' Now Accepted and Respected?

I believe that, since I first stressed the problem of capital flows and their perverse influences, most informed observers have ignored the point or have asserted that it was of little importance — even with no exchange controls.[19] Indeed, the problem was not mentioned, let alone discussed, in the Delors Report. There are, however, some signs of change — at least among those whose minds are not closed to the evidence. In January 1990, *The Economist* suggested that Italy was a working example of the 'Walters critique'.[20] I do not think that the evidence of Italy between January and June 1990 has in any way discredited the critique, and I would expect Italy to come under additional pressure now that overt exchange controls have been removed.

Even more interesting is the case of the peseta. What may be perhaps most revealing is the following extract from an article, one of whose authors was a member of the Delors Committee:

> 'The entry [into the EMS/ERM] of the Spanish peseta in June 1989 provided a foretaste of what is in store, in case sterling were to join. That step would improve confidence in the UK currency and — provided, as seems likely, that sterling interest rates remain higher than DM rates — lead to sizeable outflows from low-inflation EMS-countries to the UK. That would not be welcome in view of the already highly liquid state of the UK economy; at some point the process would be interrupted, as anticipations of realignment arise. Given the British tradition of using monetary policy in a relatively activist way for purposes of domestic

stabilization, markets would be justified in assuming that the
EMS will be in for a rougher ride than, say, in the 1987-89 period.
The system would come to look more like the view of it presented
in Walters (1986), which we tended to regard as more of a caricature when it was first put forward at a time when German
leadership was more firmly established and some capital controls
were still in place, and in other unstable models of economic
interaction between countries where inflation and nominal
interest rates have not converged closely and discrete realignments are possible.

'In such a world, capital flows can be destabilising by flowing
towards higher inflation countries, perpetuating inflation differentials and, ultimately, generating massive outflows prior to
anticipated realignments. The enlargement of membership makes
it more, not less urgent to move beyond stage one towards an
EMU with more centralised monetary management. Far from
causing offence among present EMS-members, labelling stage
one "a half-baked house" should prompt reflection on how the
system could be strengthened to accommodate sterling too.'[21]

As the authors imply, the entry of Spain into the ERM
(albeit with 6 per cent limits) sent the peseta to near the top
of the band as capital poured in to take advantage of interest
rates of around 15 per cent. The money supply has
expanded dramatically and even the most stringent limits
imposed on commercial bank lending have not stopped the
credit inflation. It has merely driven the expansion into
different forms — mainly the *pagares de empresa* or commercial
paper market, where the June 1989 interest rates were about
15 per cent. The rate of inflation has risen to 7 per cent (in
June 1990), and it seems likely that it will go on rising for
some time. The realignment will soon be anticipated. I
believe that the authors are right to use the Spanish
experience as relevant to a judgement of what would happen
if Britain joined the ERM. And, as they infer, the disruption
caused by Britain's entry would be much greater than that
associated with the peseta. Of course, I do not share the
conclusion that this necessarily increases the urgency of

proceeding to EMU. That would be *one* solution, but there are others — such as floating. All in all, however, it is gratifying to see that such authoritative and influential authors agree with my analysis of a 'half-baked' system.[22]

Covert Exchange Controls

Although overt exchange controls have been largely eliminated in the EMS, this does not mean that there is complete or even substantial freedom to move capital and currencies over borders. Continental Europe has substantial control over national banking systems and over financial institutions. These are most apparent in the cartel structures that are characteristic of banking and finance in France and Italy. French bankers concede, albeit privately, that their high margins and high costs are due to a cartellised market which the government continues to sanction because it makes it easier for government to maintain covert control.[23] Similarly, it is well known that Italian banks have extensive cartel arrangements, and that government controls percolate throughout all large banks.

Perhaps more surprising, however, is the extent of covert exchange controls in Germany — apart from Britain and perhaps the Netherlands, the most liberal member of the Community. German insurance companies, which control probably more than 70 per cent of long-term savings, are not permitted to buy non-Deutschemark denominated assets. By regulation they must have a complete currency match for their obligations. They can hold only 5 per cent of their portfolio in equities (necessarily, mark equities). In a corporatist society, the purpose of these regulations, although ostensibly prudential, is to ensure a recycling of capital, usually via the intermediation of the banks, as loans to the large firms of German industry. Similarly, there are restrictions imposed on the holdings of foreigners (that is, non-citizens of the Federal Republic) in *Bundesbankobligationen* (the German equivalent of gilts).[24]

Whatever the reason for these restrictions, the effect is to prevent the free flow of capital within the Community. They act as exchange controls, and perhaps even more effectively than conventional exchange controls, in preventing any mass flight of capital or in stemming the tide of an inflow. Even more important is their role in maintaining a corporatist system among the continental members of the Community. But that is another story.

Conclusions

The various forms of exchange rate régimes which have been practised in Europe since the Second World War have all depended on exchange controls, both overt and covert. So far the EMS is no exception. Unlike the other régimes, the EMS has persisted for more than a decade and has not yet collapsed. On the contrary, it is planned as the basis of a Monetary Union of the Community. The evidence suggests that the EMS has not been helpful in reducing inflation rates, in promoting overall exchange rate stability, in securing high growth and investment, and in stabilising interest rates. In part this may be due to the perverse incentives generated by the ERM. The essence of the ERM prevents automatic adjustment mechanisms in response to shocks, and induces perverse oscillations in monetary policy. Ironically, the ERM mechanism works well when there are the same inflation and interest rates in all countries — but, then, why bother?

EXCHANGE RATE POLICIES AND POLITICS

The Medium-Term Financial Strategy

THE EMS STARTED on 13 March 1979, and Britain was scheduled to have an election within the next three months. The economy was in a parlous state. Neither party had any intention of joining what most thought to be the offspring of a 'snake'. Experience since the breakdown of Bretton Woods had shown that it was extraordinarily difficult to maintain nominal exchange rates at levels which differed substantially from the market. The massive outflows and inflows of money in 1975-77 had made the point.

The first Thatcher Government saw its first main task as that of securing financial stability. In particular the high rate of inflation, at an underlying 15 per cent, had to be brought under control. The main instruments for bringing inflation under control were evident from the beginning: the rate of growth of the money supply, which in the first half of 1979 had been running at some 16 per cent, had to be brought down. Mr Lawson was one of the main architects of the document that set out Britain's *Medium-Term Financial Strategy* (MTFS). This envisaged a steady downward trend in the rate of monetary growth (of M3) and a decline in the fiscal deficit that was consistent with the monetary targets. If anyone suggested that Britain should tie itself through a fixed exchange rate in order to reduce inflation, I can attest that the suggestion did not get very far.

To the modern reader this may seem odd. In the many attempts that have been made to control inflation (albeit near hyperinflations) in Latin America, in Israel and now in Eastern Europe, the conventional wisdom is that the exchange rate must be controlled and usually that it should be fixed. But even in 1979-81, in France and Italy where inflation was in the teens, a fixed (or strictly pseudo-fixed) exchange rate was thought to be a central plank of a disinflationary policy. It was a way of converging on the low inflation rate of Germany. Why not in Britain? And, indeed, why not in the United States?

Fixed or Flexible?

The first answer is that, while an exchange rate fix may be useful for bringing really high inflations down, it is clearly not a necessary or even useful condition for controlling inflation rates of *circa* 10 to 20 per cent. The disinflationary policy with a flexible exchange rate will have lower costs than the policy of fixing the rate. (The evidence on the higher growth rates and lower inflation rates of the non-ERM countries reviewed in Chapter 5 is relevant here.) The argument, however, may be that one needs an anchor for the currency in order to ensure that the appropriate monetary squeeze is properly applied; one can, so to speak, trust the monetary authorities to stick to an exchange rate target whereas, because of political pressure, it is very difficult for them to pursue the appropriate policy of monetary restraint. That view is clearly not merely discredited but shown to be perverse by experience in both the UK and the USA. As we saw, both sterling and the dollar soared to new heights as the monetary squeeze took effect. If an exchange rate peg had been employed in the UK, the monetary squeeze would have been quickly reversed in order to stop sterling rising above its upper bound. The peg would have had the opposite effect on monetary policy to that which was intended.[1] The inflation would have been refuelled rather than doused.

Secondly — and this point applies to the UK only and not to the USA — Mrs Thatcher's first major act in international economic policy was to abolish exchange controls in 1979.[2] No such liberalisation would have been possible if Britain had been on a fixed-exchange rate régime. And since the effects of the abolition of exchange controls were unknown (and incidentally turned out to be quite different from forecasts), it would have been folly on a grand scale to have given any commitment to a fixed régime. It was widely argued, in addition, that Britain was a large oil producer, and one could not anticipate, nor be expected to counter, the effects of variations in the oil price on the exchange rate. For my part, I doubt whether the oil-price argument was entirely valid, or if so was at all powerful.[3] Most observers, however, believed that oil was most important, and there is no unequivocal evidence to discredit that view. So it was prudent to eschew the ERM and all its uncertainties.

The Role of the Exchange Rate, 1980-82

The exact role of the exchange rate in economic policy is subject to many subtle interpretations. During this period, however, there was a general attitude, albeit with different degrees of emphasis, to the exchange rate which was broadly shared by the civil servants and ministers. First, the exchange rate was not a target for policy. This applied to the whole range of instruments — interest rates, funding operations, and fiscal measures. All instruments were concentrated primarily on domestic targets and indicators. The exchange rate was left very largely to market forces. This did not mean that there was no intervention at all, or even that it was restricted merely to smoothing operations. The Bank of England did, on occasion, intervene in markets quite heavily, but this intervention was virtually always sterilized through the money markets. The prime purpose was to prevent what was usually called a 'free-fall' in the exchange rate having an effect on the market for gilts. But there was no target rate. Indeed, from the Budget on 10 March 1981 over the next nine months (to 11 December) the effective exchange rate fell by about 10 per cent.

Although the exchange rate was not a target, it would have been foolish simply to ignore it. The exchange rate may tell us something about the severity or laxity of monetary policy. This may be a useful indicator when, as sometimes happens, the usual indicators of monetary growth are badly distorted or for some reason unavailable. Such conditions occurred in 1981. The deregulation of financial markets caused a great growth of M3 and other broad money aggregates — the targets of the MTFS. And there was industrial action by the civil service which caused long delays in the production of the monetary statistics; but of course the exchange rate was readily available.

So the exchange rate loomed large in the discussions of policy. The decline in sterling's dollar exchange rate (about 18 per cent from 10 March to 29 September 1981) was the primary reason for raising interest rates from 12 to 16 per cent. In retrospect, the squeeze was overdone. The steep decline in narrow money (both M1 and non-interest-bearing M1) in the third quarter of 1981 undoubtedly caused a marked slowdown in the recovery in 1982. The exchange rate had misled us into the belief that the monetary laxity was far greater than it was in reality. As for the reasons for such a misleading indicator, it was like 'rounding up the usual suspects'. First, the United States had embarked on a severe monetary squeeze which made the normal dollar comparison particularly wayward; secondly, there were rumours about the price of oil; and lastly, as reflected in the opinion polls, the Government appeared to be distinctly shaky. All had a depressing effect on the exchange rate, which had nothing to do with domestic monetary policy.

From September 1981 through to October 1982 it appeared that the authorities were on an exchange rate target of sorts. The effective rate remained in the relatively small range 90 to 92 over this whole period (1975 = 100). But from the overt statistics it could have been just as readily asserted that Britain was on a Friedmanian path of stable monetary expansion. Monetary growth (M0) remained in the 2 to 5 per cent range. Indeed, all the monetary aggregates were within the target range for the financial year 1982/83.

91

Election 1983

Not only was Britain *not* on an exchange rate target; I believe that everyone, except the most absurd ideologists, knew that such a target, or even the market perception of such a target, might well be disastrous in the environment of a closely fought election. The scenario was stark. The Labour party platform was clearly to resocialise Britain. Inflationary expansion was one of its main planks. Increased taxation, renationalisation, and a substantial spread of controls were among the main instruments for change. And various promises had been made to reintroduce exchange controls and bring back much of the capital that had fled the country so that it could finance job creation at home.

Such a programme is a warning to any asset holder to get out while the going is good. The warning is the more to be heeded, the higher the Labour party scores in the opinion polls and the more it appears that the policy is expropriatory. This is a great temptation to Labour. The more socialist the policy, the greater the capital flight. If the Government were on an exchange rate target, it would have to raise interest rates — probably very sharply. But this would squeeze business, lower output and probably throw more on the dole. Not the sort of scenarios in which governments are re-elected. The alternative of avoiding the monetary squeeze and letting the exchange rate find its own depreciated level does avoid the election-induced recession.

The Government followed this strategy by letting the exchange rate fall by 15 per cent both in nominal and real terms from November 1982 to March 1983.[4] Interest rates rose by 2 percentage points, M0's growth rate was reduced, and this was enough to ensure the gentle but persistent disinflationary pressure. In the event, the run-up to the election was smooth. Although it has been claimed that devaluations do even more political damage than monetary squeezes, the 1983 election result discredits that view.

It appears that a socialist opposition has an enormous advantage in inducing capital flight, interest rate increases, and wrong-footing government economic policy. But, like most things, it can be carried too far. True, the more rabid the socialist programme, the greater the capital flight. But the more extensive the expropriation, the less the electoral support. If its purpose is to maximise the probability of gaining power, then the Labour party will pitch its programme to balance this reduction in the vote against the gain in support derived from the perversion of the government's policy. In the events of 1983, I believe that the Labour party, largely because of internal tensions, badly miscalculated the trade-off. Their programme of old-fashioned, unreconstructed socialism put off the voters so that the party never really looked as though it had a chance of gaining power.[5] The Tories won.

The EMS and the 1982 Decision

The EMS, and exchange rate targetting, had hardly figured in the election at all. Labour were far more vitriolic than any Tory about the iniquities of any Community constraint on their sovereignty. Nevertheless, in 1981 the issue of Britain's membership had been raised, largely at the behest of the existing members of the ERM.

As was widely reported in the media, in January 1982 at No. 10 Downing Street, a meeting chaired by the Prime Minister was held of the Chancellor, the Foreign Secretary, and the Governor with their advisers to consider the case for entry. It was decided that 1982 was not an appropriate time to join the ERM. Of course this did not mean that there would never be good reason to join. Circumstances may change or the ERM may change. The issue was left open; we should join only when and if it was appropriate.

That decision was fortunate. Had Britain joined the ERM at the average mark rate of 4.3 (for the first quarter of 1981), it would have required very large increases in interest rates to hold this parity.[6] Even with the 2 percentage points increase in interest rates that actually occurred, the Deutschemark rate had slipped to 3.7 by the first quarter of 1983 —

the eve of the election. But in the ERM for such a short period there would have been much reluctance to realign substantially enough to discourage the speculative capital raiders. In my judgement, if we had joined the ERM in early 1982, the pressures would have been quite insupportable.

The New Chancellor

Mr Lawson must be considered among the best prepared chancellors of the exchequer this century. As Financial Secretary in 1979-82, he had been closely involved in the Medium-Term Financial Strategy, including the introduction of indexed gilts, and the funding policy. He had also been Secretary of State for Energy in the crucial period of 1982-83.[7]

The basic policy of the Government was to continue with Sir Geoffrey Howe's gentle but persistent downward pressure on the monetary instruments to bring inflation down. The exchange rate was one of the factors to be taken into account in judging the tightness of monetary policy. But there was no targetting of the exchange rate and no shadowing of the EMS. Both these trends can be easily seen in Figures 3 and 4. The growth of M0 was on a gently declining trend from the middle of 1983, when it was about 7 per cent per annum, to the last quarter of 1986, when it was about 3 per cent. If this downward trend had been continued, the growth of the monetary base would, by the end of 1988, have been approximately zero.

In my view the policy over the period 1983-86 was about as close as one could get to ideal. The underlying inflation rate fell, with a bump or 'blip' in 1985, from about 5 per cent to some 3 per cent in 1986. Had the policy been continued, so that a zero M0 growth rate was achieved by the end of 1988 and thereafter the monetary base had remained unchanged, it is likely that the rate of inflation would also have been approximately zero. Mr Lawson had on various occasions said that the ultimate aim was to eliminate inflation completely and over the years ensure a stable price level. Here he was within two years of achieving that once elusive goal . . .[8]

Figure 3:
Growth Rates of Nominal M0: UK, 1979-89

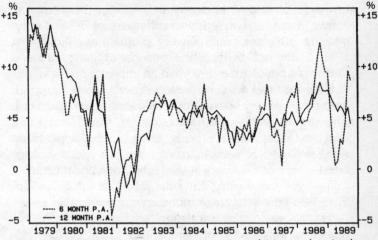

Source: Gordon Pepper, *Money, Credit and Inflation*, Research Monograph 44, London: Institute of Economic Affairs, 1990, Chart III, page 19.

Figure 4:
Sterling/Deutschemark Exchange Rate (weekly), 1979-89

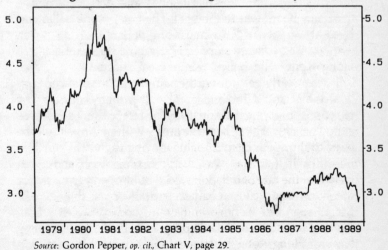

Source: Gordon Pepper, *op. cit.*, Chart V, page 29.

The Curious Case of Hong Kong, 1983

The remarkable story of how this opportunity was missed can only be related from my partial point of view. The conversion of Mr Lawson to an enthusiast for Britain's entry into the ERM took place between February and November 1985. It may well be that the experience of fixing the Hong Kong dollar in October 1983 had an influence on his views.

Until the breakdown of Bretton Woods, Hong Kong had been on a currency board with a fixed sterling exchange rate. The sterling parity was maintained by the Hong Kong Currency Board always being ready to exchange Hong Kong dollar notes against sterling notes at a fixed exchange rate. During the next decade, the Hong Kong dollar could be characterised as floating amid the jetsam of the 1970s. But there was no discipline of monetary control to replace the currency board. The escalation of the US dollar, the recession, inflation, justifiable doubts about government monetary policy, and the political uncertainties generated by the end of the lease (1997) caused a number of runs out of the Hong Kong dollar. These runs eventually culminated in a massive flight in September 1983. The Thatcher Government reacted with exemplary speed and decisiveness. The Currency Board was reinstituted. The Hong Kong dollar was fixed at a parity of 7.8 Hong Kong dollars to 1 US dollar. The run immediately stopped and capital flooded back into Hong Kong. The policy was a great success.

It was clearly best to engineer a rapid return to a currency board system. Although there were many outstanding questions — about the adequacy of Hong Kong's reserves, about whether Hong Kong's currency (the HK$) should be fixed to the dollar or to Special Drawing Rights (SDRs) (I do not think that sterling was a serious possibility), and about exactly how the Currency Board would operate — a policy decision was urgently required. The policy was duly agreed. Mr Lawson did wonder, and with good cause, why I, an avowed British floater, could be so enthusiastic in proposing a fix for Hong Kong. I explained my penchant for clarity in policy and the perils of pseudo systems. I doubt whether my explanation had any effect whatsoever, but I suspect the subsequent euphoric experience of Hong Kong did dispose Mr Lawson, and perhaps many others, to be more favourably inclined towards a pseudo-fix for sterling.

Preparing for ERM, 1985

The year 1985 began with the Chancellor saying that in monetary policy most attention should be paid to the exchange rate. However, in February he was still opposed to Britain joining the ERM at that time; but by September the media campaign to join was in full swing. Corresponding to the elevation of the exchange rate into proposed ERM entry, was the downgrading of monetary indicators. Sterling M3 had been downgraded somewhat in 1981 with some attention being given to the exchange rate. In 1982 narrow money in the form of M1 had entered the target list, and the exchange rate gained even more prominence. After M0 replaced M1 in 1984, the exchange rate was accorded primacy among monetary indicators.

This became quite clear in early 1985. Base rates were increased from 9.5 per cent in December 1984 to 14 per cent in February 1985. The reasons could not be seen in any sustained acceleration of M0. True, there was a 'spike' in December, but this was soon corrected by a trough in January (see Figure 5). Nor could one point to any clear explosive behaviour in sterling M3, PSL2 or any of the broad aggregates.[9] On the other hand, the dramatic fall in the dollar exchange rate to close to one-for-one in February (a near-20 per cent fall over the year), and the reduction of 15 per cent in the effective rate were powerful reasons for the Chancellor to impose his monetary squeeze.[10] Yet there was no question, at that time, of joining the ERM. Exchange rates were too turbulent and monetary conditions appeared to need tightening (at least according to the exchange rate interpretation).

But there is no doubt that joining the ERM at a propitious

97

Figure 5:
Base Rates and M0: UK, 1984-89

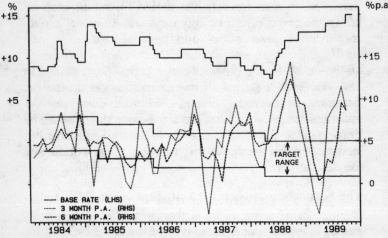

Source: Gordon Pepper, *op. cit.*, Chart IV, page 19.

time had become a central plank of the Chancellor's policy. This became clear in early June 1985. Several city commentators had been arguing that 'monetarism is dead'.[11] Were there parallels between 1972-74 and 1985- ? Retail price inflation had reached 7 per cent in May and June 1985 compared with 5.1 per cent in mid-1984. The growth rate of M3 had begun to accelerate. In their attempts to contain that growth rate, the authorities had accumulated a massive 'bill mountain', which many thought, erroneously, represented a great monetary laxity. In my view, the fact that the monetary base had been well contained (see Figure 5) was good evidence that there was no inflationary Armageddon coming in 1986-87. The absence of any take-off of inflation in asset prices, particularly land and houses, was additional evidence to support the argument that monetary policy had not been loose. In the performance of both M0 and asset prices, the situation in 1985 was quite unlike that in 1972.

But whether and when to join the ERM was another

matter on which there was no agreement. I had made my views clear in the manuscript of my *Britain's Economic Renaissance*. But so far as I was aware, there had been no critical discrediting of my arguments about capital movements, exchange controls, and perverse policies. I had conceded the argument that the ERM could be a *discipline* on *any* government (the possibility of a Labour government in 1987-88 was not all that remote at that time), and on wage demands by powerful unions. Although this case had superficial plausibility, I did not see that membership of the ERM had *in fact* given rise to any more stiffening of government sinews, compared with countries outside the ERM.

The October-November 1985 Attempt to Enter the ERM

During the next few months, the Treasury and the Bank prepared the arguments for and against entry into the ERM. By November the inflation rate had subsided to 5.5 per cent and was expected (and did) fall to about 2.5 per cent by June 1986. One of the conditions for ease of entry had been satisfied. The mark-sterling exchange rate had been fairly stable over 1984. But 1985 was a year of great instability. The rate of DM3.5 in February was clearly reckoned to be too low and a threat to anti-inflationary policy. By July 1985 it had exceeded DM4; this was thought to be too high and put too much pressure on industry. In early November the rate had slipped to half-way between these two values, at DM3.75.

It was argued that joining the ERM (and I believe everyone had in mind the narrow band of plus or minus 2.25 per cent) would reinforce the counter-inflationary strategy. It would be not only an anchor but an observable and credible anchor. Businessmen would know that they could not look to a slide in the exchange rate to bail them out of their own mismanagement. This, of course, was a repeat of the 1982 brief. But an additional difficulty now was the waywardness of the monetary targets, particularly

99

sterling M3.[12] (In fact, the misleading nature of M3 had been argued by me from the end of 1980 and thereafter.) Monetary policy was said to be becoming very difficult to present in a credible form. An exchange rate target would solve all such psychological and presentational difficulties. Thus solved, there would be such an effusion of confidence in the conduct of the authorities that the uncertainty premium attached to interest rates would fall.[13] Much weight was placed on the additional stability in the (Deutschemark) exchange rate through expectations generated by the ERM, and there would be less room for speculation. The counter-arguments, of course, had already appeared (for example, in my *Britain's Economic Renaissance*) and, in spite of the limited coverage by the media, I imagine they were also again reviewed by the authorities.

What If Britain Had Entered the ERM in 1985?

It is interesting to reflect on what would have happened if Britain had entered the ERM in early or mid-November 1985. The parity or central rate at which one enters a fixed exchange rate system is always a critical decision — as Churchill found in 1925, the Chileans discovered in 1979, and Hong Kong observed in 1983. We can get some idea of what would have happened if Britain had entered the ERM at DM3.75 by observing what actually happened to the mark-sterling rate from November 1985. By the end of December the rate had sagged to DM3.53, by mid-1986 to DM3.00, and by the end of 1986 it was hovering around DM2.80. In 13 months sterling had fallen by about 27 per cent.

In order to give some idea of the effect of the ERM on Britain's policy I shall assume that there was no realignment in the first year or so of entry. The DM3.75 rate is held. The question is, then, how far would interest rates have to rise in order to hold the central rate at that level? Some estimates can be made by applying the so-called '4 to 1' rule, namely that a 4 per cent depreciation in the exchange rate is counterbalanced by a 1 per cent increase in base rate.[14] This would imply that holding the ERM central value at 3.75 would have required increases of (27/4) 6.75 percentage points in interest rates over and above the 10 to 12.5 per cent that were in effect throughout. This would have implied interest rates of some 17 to 20 per cent.

Many EMS protagonists would claim that this estimate does not take account of the beneficial effects on expectations, including the greater certainty and credibility of being in the ERM.[15] It seems dangerous to rely so much on a subject we know so little about, namely expectations. But, in any case, exchange rate pressure which induced such high interest rates would clearly generate expectations of realignment or perhaps even withdrawal or, worse still, of incipient exchange controls.

'A Godsend'

In retrospect, the widely reported intransigence of the Prime Minister to entering the ERM was a godsend. If we had entered, then raising interest rates to new highs in late 1985 and throughout 1986 would have jeopardised, even ruined, the Conservative party's prospects in the election of 1987. After such a very tight monetary squeeze throughout 1986, there would have been a recession — and most likely a deep one — in 1987-88. This would have been exacerbated by the capital flight and escalation of interest rates discussed above. In that event, the Government would no doubt have taken some evasive action, such as realignment, as the dire consequences of the decision to join the ERM became apparent. But, willy-nilly, any such actions would be acknowledgement of an error of policy, and hardly a basis for asking for another term in government.

It is easy to conclude that Mrs Thatcher was lucky in just happening to be right. Alternatively, the market exchange rate might have remained more or less constant and so there would have been no trouble in maintaining the ERM central rate up to the election. Before mellowing with such

101

comforting thoughts, one should review the history of exchange rates since 1982 (see Figure 4). There are few periods where one could describe the exchange rate as being stable without a pronounced drift. (We must acknowledge, however, that 1984 was *relatively* stable, with a small drift from near DM4.0 to DM3.5 — a near-13 per cent devaluation.) Alternatively, the underlying market exchange rate might just have gone the other way and massively appreciated. But, as we shall see in 1987-88, this is exactly what did happen and, with the 'shadowing' of the Deutschemark, this delivered a substantial inflation in 1989.

The 'End of Monetarism', 1986

Without the restrictions imposed by the ERM, 1986 was a good year. Growth was about 3.5 per cent and inflation was way down, partly because of the collapse of the oil price and partly because of the reductions in mortgage interest rates. (It is curious that few commentators observed the coincidence of the collapse of the Deutschemark exchange rate and the *fall*, rather than the rise, of the rate of inflation.) But even as early as 1986 the writing was, albeit faintly, on the wall.

At various stages since 1983 the Chancellor had announced that the ultimate objective was stability of the price level — that is to say, zero inflation. Indeed, the policy of joining the ERM was thought to be consistent with this aim, since the objective of the Bundesbank, too, was a stable price level. A stable price level required a reduction in the rate of growth of M0 from its ambient 3 to 5 per cent in 1985 to zero. This monetary growth path consistent with the objective of zero inflation by 1990 can be adduced from Figure 3; by 1988 the quantity of M0 must be stable, and its growth rate zero. From 1983 to mid-1986 the trend rate of growth of M0 was gently declining and, had it continued to decline at that rate, the goal of zero inflation would have been reached in 1990. The actual record, however, shows a marked increase of some 2 percentage points in the second half of 1986.

At least as far as M0 is concerned, this increase marked a turning point in the policy of persistent pursuit of lower inflation which had been manifest since the 1983 election. It was not a dramatic reversal. The change was initially small, almost imperceptible. Yet, as can be seen in Figure 3, the divergence between a target path of zero inflation by 1990 and the actual growth rate of M0 expanded inexorably throughout 1987 and 1988. Finally, in September 1988, the growth rate of M0 rose to over 8 per cent and its divergence from the zero-inflation path grew to as much as 7 percentage points.

If ever one is to put a date on the 'end of monetarism', then I think the middle of 1986 has a good claim. Of course it may be argued that this was nothing more than the usual pre-election expansion to give the voters an aura of prosperity in which, it is hoped, they will re-elect the incumbents. But it was more than that. The boost persisted for three years, long after the election.

There are many possible explanations for this change in policy. First, there were growing doubts about the relevance of the monetary aggregates. Although Treasury officials had demonstrated that M0 was an efficient guide for monetary policy, various commentators had repeated that the City could not conceivably regard such small change as an appropriate target. If the City could ignore M0, why not the Chancellor? Similarly, one could explain away the burgeoning broader aggregates and particularly sterling M3. In a financial system that was changing its very structure so dramatically, M3 was a dog that had barked too often to be taken seriously. But I suspect that the most seductive influence was the general attitude among the Group of Five (G5) finance ministers[16] that exchange rates were too important to be left to the whims of markets. All right-thinking finance ministers agreed on the need to topple the dollar in 1985 — hence the Plaza agreement. Among the G5, Mr Lawson was clearly the most clever and the most experienced. It must have been quite heady stuff to redraw the financial map of the world. And Mr Lawson must have connected the Plaza and Louvre exchange rate targetting on a global scale with the domestic problem of the UK.

The Untarnished Attraction of the EMS

So it must have appeared the logical next step to take Britain into the ERM and, most importantly, to play a full role as the second most important financial power in Europe, first in influencing the policy of the Bundesbank and, secondly, as the honest broker between Germany and France in developing an integrated financial system for Europe. All these considerations might explain the persistence of the drive, by hook or by crook, to get Britain into the ERM.

In this endeavour, Mr Lawson had powerful allies. The banking community was quite firmly in his camp, although some managers were worried about the effects on interest rate variability. The City was said to be enthusiastic for a fixed mark parity and entry into the ERM, no doubt because City arbitrageurs relished a safe bet at realignments. The CBI had stated clearly its full and complete support for entry. This at least offset the much more sceptical view coming from the management of industry — the Institute of Directors. And above all, as a highly successful reforming Chancellor, Mr Lawson had fulsome support on the Conservative benches in the House of Commons.

In view of the behaviour of the sterling-mark exchange rate in 1985-86, and the obvious difficulties Britain would have encountered had she joined at the November rate of DM3.75, one would have thought that this would have given the Chancellor pause before saddling up for another ride on the tiger. Clearly it did not. Nor can I find any satisfactory explanation for ignoring the lessons of 1985-86. It is inconceivable that the Treasury official did not carry out 'what if ...?' exercises on this period.[17] I suppose he may have surveyed the evidence and drawn quite different conclusions from those which I have adduced above. For example, accepting the facts as I outlined them, he may have believed that the magic ingredient of expectations and confidence would clearly bail sterling out of any difficulties, as had apparently happened in Italy, notwithstanding Britain's open financial markets. But what is more likely is that he ignored the economic arguments on the ground — alas, not unjustified — that the economists had usually been useless in predicting exchange rate movements. He may have felt more at home with his hunches.

'Shadowing' the Mark

And his hunches, tactically, were good. When sterling began 'shadowing' the mark in early 1987, the Deutschemark rate had fallen below 2.8, even though base rates were relatively high at 11 per cent. Indeed, at this value the mood of the market was that sterling had reached its bottom. A policy to maintain the rate at around DM3.0 was both attractive and easy. Indeed, it was combined with a fall in base rates from 11 per cent at the turn of the year to 9 per cent before the election in May. Sterling soon appreciated in February to DM2.9 and thereafter it rarely deviated more than 1.5 per cent (0.05 Deutschemark) from DM3.0.

The economic ambience of this policy seemed like a new golden age. Growth proceeded at between 4 and 6 per cent, according to the measure used. Investment boomed with a 7 per cent growth. Inflation remained low, a little over 4 per cent, but the tax price index was only about 2.5 per cent. A great tax reform was introduced in the March 1987 budget and continued in the budget of 1988. Marginal personal tax rates were reduced to a maximum of 40 per cent, and many loopholes and anomalies were swept away. Yet, such was the ebullience of the economy that revenue increased dramatically and the deficit in the public sector turned into a surplus. Debt retirement began. Interest rates fell.

The pre-tax real rate of return on assets in the corporate sector had been rising since 1981 (when it was 2 per cent) and by the end of 1987 it had reached 12 per cent. It was expected to rise even further, and so it did — to over 13 per cent in 1989. Such high rates of return had not been seen since 1964. More importantly, they clearly exceeded the rates of return in other OECD countries.[18] Much of this improvement was due to supply-side changes, which were expected to continue.[19] This meant that there was a great attraction for investors, both domestic and foreign, to invest in Britain, either through foreign direct investment or portfolios. The demand for sterling was boosted by this investment effect. There was perhaps an even larger demand created by the interest differential between the United Kingdom and overseas. In January 1987, United States treasury bills were yielding only 5.85 per cent compared with about 11 per cent on sterling bills. The risks of a three-month devaluation of sterling were clearly low, so sterling attracted many buyers.

The increase in the demand for sterling buoyed up the exchange rate at DM3.00; there was initially no difficulty in holding it there. The authorities did intervene largely to prevent the rate rising above the 3.0 limit. This took the form of selling sterling and buying convertible currencies. Intervention statistics remain a secret. (It is interesting to note, however, that during 1987 the convertible currency reserves increased from $13.78 billion to $35.73 billion. One may conjecture that much of the increase was in anticipation of a need to prepare for the defence of a pegged exchange rate whether in or out of the ERM.[20]) The intervention was formally sterilized in the sense that it was not allowed to have any persistent direct impact on the money market rates of interest. Bills were sold to take sterling off the market. Thus the bill mountain, such a source of concern in 1985, melted away.

Many studies have shown that sterilized intervention has little lasting effect on exchange rates. Since most of it was sterilized in 1987, the persistent pressure for an appreciation of sterling continued. The only way to prevent it was a reduction in interest rates relative to those in other OECD countries. First, however, there was a little diversion due to the Louvre (February 1987) agreement. In May the United States authorities were driven to raise interest rates sharply to stop the decline of the dollar (again after a failure of massive internationally co-ordinated sterilized intervention to do the trick). US rates continued to rise throughout the year until the stock market crash of 19 October. In July British interest rates were increased by 1 per cent, but thereafter they did not follow the dollar up further. And following the October crash, base rates resumed their downward path to 8.5 per cent at the end of 1987.

It is ironic that during 1987, the attempt to put a floor under the dollar and the attempt to put a cap on sterling both failed. Both were fought with the biggest intervention funds ever deployed. Both substantially sterilized their intervention, and discovered it was ineffective. Both were driven back to monetary policy, to higher interest rates in the United States and to lower ones in Britain.[21]

The massive interventions in Britain came to an end in the first months of 1988. It was rumoured that more than $2 billion was spent on intervention in one day. Intervention was scaled back to the normal smoothing operations. There was a well-publicised disagreement between the Chancellor and the Prime Minister. Just before the March budget, the Prime Minister made it clear that you 'cannot buck the market'. That was manifestly true. In any case, the ability of sterling to maintain its DM3.0 fix ended on 4 March, and by the end of the month it had risen to over DM3.12.

The October Excuse

But this did not mark the end of the expansionary policy. In a vain attempt to put a somewhat higher cap on the exchange rate, interest rates were reduced again to their low of 7.5 per cent in May 1988. The only conceivable rationalisation for such a policy was that the exchange rate appreciation, both overt and incipient, showed that monetary policy was still 'too tight'. Yet every other indicator

107

suggested that monetary policy was too loose rather than too tight. The labour market was showing distinct signs of strain and unemployment was falling by about 50,000 a month. The prices of assets — particularly real estate — were rising strongly. The current balance of payments had turned markedly into the red, and there was a clear import boom. Investment boomed ahead at record rates. The monetary indicators were all pointing to an inflationary surge. The M0 figures suggested that there would be a 2 per cent increase in underlying inflation coming in 1988-89, and the broader money aggregates were suggesting even more alarming forecasts of price inflation. *Only* the exchange rate could be adduced as evidence that monetary policy was still 'too tight'.

What possible excuses could there be for ignoring this weight of evidence? One such excuse, according to *The Economist*, and many other supporters of the monetary expansion, is that monetary ease was the appropriate response to the 19 October 1987 crash. By this means we would then avoid the mistakes made following the crashes of 1929 and 1931. But the appropriate response to a crash is not inflationary expansion. The problem in October might well have been a run on the banking system or some other form of liquidity run. This calls for the central bank to stand ready to discount paper at penal rates to stem the run, not to flood the market with cheap money. In the event, the Federal Reserve Board of the United States handled the October crash in an exemplary manner which should have been a model for the United Kingdom. In the *Economic Report* of the President of February 1988, it was shown (page 39) that, in spite of October's troubles, the Fed actually *tightened* monetary policy in 1987 — because it feared that the expansionary policies of 1986 would promote inflation. This is exactly what was required in the United Kingdom.[22] There was nothing that prevented such a prudent policy being pursued. The Governor in his Durham speech in April 1990 observed that there had been errors of policy. I agree.

The Monetary Squeeze, June 1988 Onwards

From June 1988 monetary policy was successively tightened by raising interest rates frequently but by only half a percentage point. This was new. Normally in a squeeze the interest rate is put up substantially — usually by 2 percentage points. Then the market is much less certain about the next move of interest rates, whereas using the innovation of Mr Lawson, the market was certain of the direction of the next interest rate movement. By August base rates had been raised to 12 per cent.

But the question remained: Were the authorities *still* operating with an exchange rate band as the target? Although the band had been moved to DM3.1 to 3.3 or so, the rate was kept in that band until September 1989. But the evidence of incipient inflation became more evident with every passing day. House prices were booming, unemployment was falling as fast as ever, and labour shortages were spreading — all the signs of overheating were there for anyone to see. The need for a substantial increase in interest rates, whatever the exchange rate consequences, was manifest. Fortunately, the exchange rate pressure was reversed and became downwards and so provided a convenient argument for increasing interest rates in 1 percentage steps from 12 per cent in November 1988 to 15 per cent one year later. Thus, at last, there was the coincidence of the exchange rate giving an appropriate direction to monetary policy.[23] The market became quite convinced that it was virtually only concern about the Deutschemark and German interest rates that was driving interest rate policy in the UK. Indeed, the Chancellor and the Governor had given the market good reason for believing that exchange rates were the main determinant of interest rates.[24] And once the belief is ingrained in market lore, it is very costly to try and change it.

Britain was on the back of the tiger. As the exchange rate fell, or threatened to fall, in the Autumn of 1989, so the interest rate was driven up by market expectations. The authorities had the choice of validating expectations or changing them. However desirable it might be to avoid riding the tiger, the alternative was to fall into its jaws. The Government would certainly have been chewed up if it had announced a substantial change in its macro-economic targets. Even though 15 per cent interest rates may seem like riding the tiger into a recession, the alternative was even worse.[25]

The Foreign Exchange Reserves

So far we have ignored the consequences, particularly the costs, of fixing the exchange rate on the foreign exchange reserves. One of the little known consequences of the first Thatcher Government's financial programme was the privatisation of a substantial fraction of the official foreign exchange reserves. In 1979-80 the authorities held more than $18 billion in convertible currencies.[26] By 1984 this had been run down to about $7.5 billion. This reduction was possible because the authorities did not need substantial reserves if sterling were floating. If it were a free or pure float, then, apart from those required for normal operations, there is no need for any official reserves. But Britain was on a 'dirty' float and the Bank always liked to smooth the path of sterling, so some balances were needed for these operations.

We can conjecture that if Britain joined the ERM, then considerably more reserves would be required. One notes that France and Italy maintained reserves of 18 and 23 per cent of their exports in 1984, whereas Britain's reserves were only 6.5 per cent. It is reasonable to suppose that, were Britain to join the ERM, reserves of about three to four times the $7.5 billion, that is, $22.5 billion to $30 billion (for 1984 export volumes and in 1984 prices), would be required. Bringing them up to 1989 values, one would arrive at required reserves of $30 billion to $40 billion. (Just to confirm this figure, in 1988 the official reserves rose to $40 billion at the end of July and to over $42 billion by the end of the year.) The ERM, therefore, would require us to have

Central Bank foreign reserves have an
opportunity cost vs. domestic reserves —
depends on the form of domestic assets

additional reserves of some $20 billion to $30 billion; I shall
assume hereinafter that the extra reserves amount to $25
billion.[27]

What are the costs of keeping reserves of this size? The
real rate of return on the reserves is roughly the real short-
term interest rates in the money markets of New York and,
to a lesser extent, Frankfurt and Tokyo; a figure of around 2
per cent seems appropriate as the average value of the return
to be expected. If these funds had not been required for
padding the reserves, they would have been employed by
the private sector, as in 1980-84, as capital assets. We know
that the average real rate of return on capital employed in
private industrial and commercial companies in the UK in
1988 was about 12 per cent.[28] If these were the rates of return
of alternative investments forgone, then the cost of the
reserves was about 10 per cent of the $25 billion, or $2.5
billion a year. Of course, the alternatives forgone may be
overseas investment, either in portfolio form or in the
acquisition of real assets or direct capital formation. We do
not know the full rate of return on these investments, mainly
because of the lack of information on capital gains.[29] But
from the information available, it appears that over the
Thatcher years the rate of return has been very high at some
15 to 20 per cent, and substantially larger than that on
domestic investment. Thus the cost of the reserves for the
ERM is between $2.5 billion and $5 billion (or between £1.5
billion and £3.0 billion).

Thus, in maintaining these additional reserves, the ERM
will cost us some 0.5 to 1 per cent of GNP each year.
Whether this is considered large or small depends on the
alternatives. One possible alternative is to go the whole hog
and switch to a Deutschemark currency or to a currency
board system. (This is the logical consequence of Delors
stage 2.) Instead of pound notes, Deutschemark notes would
circulate and we would be on a full Deutschemark standard.
The Bundesbank would hold reserves; we would simply
hold some of their currency. At present, currency and coin in

the UK amount to about £17 billion, or some $26 billion. This capital value of the seignorage[30] is about the same as the additional reserves for joining the ERM.

If a currency board substitutes sterling currency at a fixed rate for Deutschemark notes, then the $26 billion equivalent can be at least partly invested in short-term mark financial assets. So the cost of the ERM is about the same as the cost of a full currency board system.

Conclusion on the Lawson Years

There is no doubt that it was an error to launch a country that had suffered much in quelling, if not conquering, inflation in 1979-82 into a renewed inflation in 1988-90. Opinions differ on when this inflationary policy started; some trace it back to 1985 with the surge in the growth of sterling M3, others only to 1987 or even 1988. But in prospect the warning signs were flashing in 1987 and were clearly bright red in the first months of 1988. I believe, however, that there is substantial agreement that the inflationary pressure could have been reduced if Mr Lawson had pursued more monetary stringency in 1987-88.

The role of the exchange rate in the general conduct of monetary policy and in particular the 'shadowing' of the mark was quite critical in exacerbating the inflationary pressure. The ambient influences arising from the Plaza and the Louvre agreements and the crash of October 1987 no doubt much affected the authorities' decisions, yet they cannot serve as an excuse. The primary motive for the expansionary policy was to contain the exchange rate at DM3.0. This was the main explanation for the inflationary policy of the latter half of 1987 through to the summer of 1988. The inflationary pressures then became too obvious to ignore, and so the long-delayed monetary squeeze began, but was not fully in place until October 1989. On normal expectations, one would not expect to see any turnaround in the rate of inflation until the turn of the year 1990/91.

Although it is not possible to venture any estimate of the

costs of the policy errors (as the Governor called them), it is possible to measure the direct costs of the additional reserves required to defend a pegged rate. These were approximately £1.5 billion to £3.0 billion or $2.5 billion to $5.0 billion. This is roughly equivalent to 1 to 2 pence off the basic rate of income tax. And it would be the direct 'reserves' cost of Britain's entry into the ERM.

A MONETARY CONSTITUTION FOR EUROPE?

Introduction

IN THIS FINAL CHAPTER, I shall try my hand at sketching a monetary system which will ensure stability of the general price level. This is what Western Europe enjoyed under the gold standard for centuries, albeit in a wobbly sort of way. The norm for a civilised society was a stable currency, not inflation. After these many decades of depreciating currencies, it seems that the world yearns again for that ancient stability. Anchors are needed. Institutions such as the Federal Reserve Board, the (old) Bank of England, and the Bundesbank have provided such anchors in various periods of the historical record. But all have, at times and to varying degrees, failed to deliver that rigidity when under pressure.

Rather than relying on authorities and institutions, one would prefer to rely on *rules*. It is rather easier to agree on rules and procedures than to agree on policies and outcomes. Furthermore, the rules should be transparent and unavoidable, rather than, as under the later gold standard, obscure and escapable. In this chapter I shall discuss the problems and prospects of basing a European currency on a commodity basket. Thus, one unit of money will always be able to purchase certain quantities of commodities which represent the budgets of consumers. I shall also consider some paths from the present situation to the commodity currency, and how commodity money may exist side by side with present national monies and European Currency Units (ECUs).

This is not, of course, a complete monetary plan for Europe. It is merely a mixture of some ingredients of a monetary constitution. It is really only half-formed. But it is proposed simply to test the ideas, not to be inflicted forthwith on suffering humanity! The underlying spirit of these ideas is that the people of Europe should be free to choose whatever currency they wish in order to carry out their business. Governments should impose neither restrictions nor penalties. Competition between currencies is the best way of preserving both our freedoms and reliable units of account. But also, in co-operation with the private sector, the governments of the Community should promote a monetary unit which, by virtue of its own operating rules, is free from inflation.

The Need for a Stable Currency

Money performs three basic functions: it serves as (i) a store of value, (ii) a unit of account, and (iii) the medium of exchange. Inflation erodes all three functions, but to very different degrees. As we know from the history of many inflations, money still serves as an intermediator in exchange even when inflation is very high. For example, in the many Latin American inflations that have occurred in the 1980s, although the increase in the price index may be as much as 30 per cent *per month*, the currency is still used for the host of small household transactions. But no-one keeps notes as a store of value and virtually all contracts are calculated, not in terms of the currency as a unit, but in US dollars or perhaps in some agreed indexed form of money.[1] The separation of the unit of account from the rapidly depreciating medium of exchange involves considerable costs — as anyone who has lived in Argentina, Brazil, *et al.*, can readily testify. One's main business is to minimise any currency holdings so that one is not substantially expropriated by the State. And it seems that *everyone* gives up many a useful employment to become a currency dealer. The main business is getting rid of currency as quickly as possible!

Maintaining a constant unit of account is as important as maintaining constant standards of physical measurement — where a kilogramme and a metre are always the same. This

115

constancy is more difficult with money because, unlike distance or weight at sea level, there is no natural and immutable definition of the value of a monetary unit. Money exchanges against a host of goods and services. In the past the definition of money has been in the form of goods, such as ounces of silver or gold of specified purity. Thus there has usually been only *one* particular good, defined and widely used as money. This is ideal only when the price of gold (say) in terms of representative baskets of other goods and services in the economy does not much change. Then gold is a good surrogate for all goods. But, over the years, gold has not behaved so well. Gold discoveries and new technologies have reduced the price of gold relative to other goods, and so induced inflation. At other times, the stocks of monetary gold have stagnated while the production of other goods has increased, and this has resulted in many years of deflation. The legendary stability of the gold standard is indeed legend. Allan Meltzer has shown that predictability of the price level and GNP was far, far less under the gold standard than under the floating rate system of the 1970s.[2] Little wonder that Keynes described gold as a 'barbarous relic'!

A Broad Commodity Money

The natural question to ask is whether it would be wise to include more goods in the definition of the monetary unit. Other precious metals are obvious candidates. Bimetallism, for example, became an active issue in Britain in the 1850s as people became concerned about the gold discoveries inducing inflation. Bimetallism involves fixing the ratio of the prices of gold and silver at the mint — and both are given the status of legal tender. Under propitious circumstances — in particular where the mint ratio is approximately the same as the free metal price ratio — the bimetal standard can function as such. But if, for example, many new, easily accessible silver deposits are discovered, then the price of silver will fall relative to that of gold, and so silver currency will drive out gold; at the fixed mint ratio, Gresham's Law works — bad

money drives out good. This is the normal fate of bimetallism.[3] Nevertheless, throughout history the periods of
bimetallism have exhibited much more stability than those
of gold monometallism.[4]   *Symmetalism*

An obvious way out of the Gresham's Law effect is to
avoid fixing the mint ratio. The unit can be defined simply as
a basket of the two metals — say, one ounce of silver and
0.02 ounces of fine gold. The price ratio could then
fluctuate. The coins would be composed of an alloy of gold
and silver in the fixed ratio. No doubt there are many
technical difficulties in minting and maintaining such coins.
But for our modern economies this does not matter since we
circulate bits of paper rather than coin. Under this metallic
commodity standard, the currency note would be a claim to
the 1/0.02 ounce mix of the metals. The monetary authorities
would stand ready to convert notes into the metal mix, and
vice versa. This requires the authorities to hold stocks of
silver and gold sufficient to meet all demands for convertibility. Any shortfall of such stocks will be reflected in
people's suspicion that the authorities will not honour their
obligations, and that the currency will become inconvertible.
There have been too many cases in history where convertibility has been suddenly revoked to allow a monetary
authority to get away with small stocks of the precious
metals.

A Commodity Money Without Commodities

The idea of a commodity money that is not based on the
narrow basis of silver or gold stocks, but is founded on a
broad range of representative commodities or services, has
surfaced periodically in discussions about monetary anchors.
The attraction of convertibility into a basket of commodities,
or even services, is that one avoids the idiosyncracies of gold
or silver supplies and all the political problems associated
with the gold producers or owners. Furthermore, it seems
quite absurd for scarce resources to be devoted to digging a
hole in the ground to extract gold, only to return that gold

117

again to the deep vaults of the world's central banks. Convertibility into the ordinary useful commodities of trade appears much more attractive as an anchor in the real economy.

The commodity basket must, of course, be very large to accommodate the normal lot sizes of wholesale trade. Similarly, the commodities must be readily storable and of identified uniform quality, in the same way that, under the gold standard, the gold content was of a given purity. And the monetary authority would clearly enter the lists as a major commodity dealer.

The prospects of a monetary authority sitting on large stocks of commodities, and the likelihood that one would add to the present grain mountains, cheese hills and wine lakes, have been sufficient to chill the enthusiasm of most of mankind. Yet some economists have also been entranced by the prospect of introducing a world Commodity Reserve Currency to replace the old role of gold and one which would, in addition, enable the world authorities to intervene massively in 'smoothing' the oscillations in commodity prices and thus reduce variations in the incomes of producers of primary commodities.[5] (Perhaps the main motive was to foster large intergovernmental transfers from the Western countries to the Third World. But as we know from the fortunes of Messrs Mobutu and Marcos, this often takes the form of transfers from poor taxpayers in rich countries to the rich rulers of poor countries.)

Indexed Reserve Asset

It has, however, also occurred to many economists (although I believe Irving Fisher was the first to enunciate the idea) that one does not really require commodities as the reserve asset.[6] Instead one could simply redeem the currency by supplying a financial asset which gave the holder sufficient resources to buy the commodities if he so wished.[7] The point is that the value of the currency will be preserved through its convertibility into a reserve asset which has a value defined as constant in terms of the commodity basket. If, for example, one defined the reserve asset in terms of a fixed fraction of the basket of goods and services that enter into the retail price index, then one unit of the currency, convertible into the reserve asset, would be of a sufficient value to purchase that fraction of the basket.

The indexed-reserve asset appears to be closely analogous to an indexed gilt-edged security. But there is a crucial difference. An indexed gilt has a fixed maturity, usually many years, at which time the principal is repaid duly enlarged in proportion to the change in the retail price index. But the authorities do *not* guarantee to redeem the gilt at par, duly uprated for the retail price index, at *any* time. With an indexed gilt, one takes one's chance on whatever price one can get in the market for such bonds. For this commodity money, the authorities always redeem at slightly below the par value of the retail price index. The 'slightly below' condition is to ensure that there is some disincentive against too ready redemption, and that the issuing authority earns sufficient profits to pay for the costs of operating the system.

A Stable Commodity Money for Europe

How would one provide this alternative of a stable European money? I believe that it should be introduced as a parallel currency to the existing national monies in Europe. In accordance with the liberal principles nominally embraced by the Community, all citizens should be allowed freely to use whatever currency they would wish, with no restraints of legal tender or overt and covert exchange controls. Thus they should be able to hold and transact in the commodity money. People would then be able to choose to conduct their business in any of the national monies or in the Euro-commodity money, the ECOM. With parallel national monies, the reserve assets, duly indexed, could be denominated in any of the member-currencies, or, if desired, in terms of a basket such as the ECU.

119

Redempt. med = any currency

There are many feasible alternative redemption arrangements, but some principles are fairly clear. First, one would restrict redemption operations to wholesale quantities of money. Thus instead of exchanging ECOM against sterling, one would specify that the ECOM would be exchanged only for large treasury bills (say, of £10,000 sterling or its equivalent). An ECOM note would be printed with the promise that

> 'This note is redeemable for a fraction (or number) of treasury bill(s) sufficient to purchase the basket of goods defined as one ECOM'.

To see how the system would work, imagine that it started during a nice equilibrium, but then that some external shock occurred, such as an increase in the price of oil, which brought inflationary pressure in its wake. Prices in ECOMs would then rise as people got rid of their ECOMs by spending them on goods and services. But the ECOMs are worth more than their value at the inflated prices, since they can be exchanged for an amount of treasury bills equivalent to the base value of the ECOM, and these treasury bills are worth more than the ECOM notes by the amount of the price rise. So people will be induced to redeem their ECOM notes; they will take their ECOMs to the European Investment Bank (EIB) and receive treasury bills in exchange. This will reduce the quantity of ECOMs and therefore depress the ECOM prices of goods, until equilibrium is again restored with the ECOM value in the market at its original goods value.[8] In this way private arbitrage will help to restore the value of the ECOM.

As an illustration, suppose that the reserve asset is an ECOM-denominated treasury bill (TB). The private sector will hold both ECOM TBs and ECOM notes. The holdings of notes will depend primarily on the transactions demand for money. The TBs, lacking the moneyness of notes (and in large denominations), will command an interest rate determined by market conditions — that is to say, the yield

≡ interest rate rule? ωn = ṗ?

on alternative assets, whether nominal or indexed. With the indexed character of the TB one would expect that the market rate of interest would be quite low — perhaps 1 or 2 per cent. Let us begin in equilibrium where people are content with their existing holdings of TBs and notes. But then an exogenous inflationary shock occurs, and the ECOM note would tend to decline in value, say by 1 per cent. But the indexed TB of 10,000 ECOMs denomination is now worth 10,100 ECOMs *and* these uprated TBs can still be purchased at a price of 10,000 ECOM *notes*. Hence the incentive for the private sector to convert their notes into TBs.[9]

TB's now at longer discount

Problems with the ECOM

There are obviously a host of problems in setting up an ECOM. Many of them are basic policy issues. For example, I have discussed linking the ECOM to the consumer basket — and, of course, I have in mind the weighted average consumer basket in the Community. The ECOM would be kept in line with the weighted average of retail price indices. This would have the advantage that no single country would have any incentive, in addition to those they already have, to distort the index. But there would also be the problem of 'harmonising' the indices and, preferably, calculating them more frequently than the present monthly figures.

A more substantive issue is whether the retail basket is an appropriate anchor. It is probably better to index to the prices of things produced, rather than consumed, by the Community; then, as with indexed gilts, holders of ECOMs would not be shielded against changes in the terms of trade. But the retail price indices are much used throughout the Community and represent a more accepted unit of standardisation of value.

In order to set up the EIB, the various central banks would contribute reserve assets, defined as outlined above, in exchange for shares on a pro-rata GDP basis. This would be analogous to the introduction of indexed gilts in the UK, and it would be best to begin with a relatively modest issue of ECOMs — though there would need to be sufficient to give proper momentum to the market. In its constitution the EIB would have the sole role of issuing and redeeming ECOMs.

An External Eurocurrency?

It might be efficacious if there was to be developed first an *external* eurocurrency, as suggested by Jacques Riboud.[10] This, in M Riboud's proposal, would be a market in constant-value dollars. The Community could encourage this market and guide it by suggesting that the standard of value should be related to the weighted retail (or producer) price index for the Community. The ECOM could then take over the external unit of account, accepted and even hallowed by use, and internalise it.

There is no doubt that creating an ECOM would not ease the task of the constituent monetary authorities in dealing with the liberation of financial markets to which all member-countries are committed. But it is doubtful if it would make the task much more difficult. If, for example, Greeks can transact in Deutschemarks rather than drachmas, the possibility of substituting ECOMs would not entail a great change. As people in Greece switched out of depreciating drachmas into either Deutschemarks or ECOMs, the Greek monetary authorities would have to reduce their drachma monetary expansion in order to keep inflation at its existing rate.

The value of the ECOM is preserved through ECOM *currency* being expanded or contracted according to demand arbitrageurs. But, of course, currency is the small change of any modern monetary system. As we know, notwith-standing the success of this form of currency board control in Hong Kong, the City is most sceptical of any such form of control being effective. It remains to be seen whether the note issue of ECOMs would be sufficient for control.

An ECOM Monopoly for the Community?

If there is to be a monetary union which develops, as Delors envisaged, through the EMS becoming more stringent, that is to say, with narrower bands and virtually no realignments, then it must be based on the dominant role of a reunified Germany. There are obvious political objections to this arrangement, which Delors tried to solve by building up a central bank of Europe (a European System of Central Banks) which would control Europe's monetary policy. But the Bundesbank, along with Britain, has strongly resisted any encroachment on its powers and prerogatives. In fact, the Bundesbank must become the main agent of European monetary control.

The reluctance of countries to surrender their monetary sovereignty to another sovereign state is entirely understandable. And this must be an especial concern if that state is a Greater Germany — so much the dominant power in the Community. It is, however, a different matter if monetary sovereignty is surrendered not to a state but to the standard of an inflation-free currency. The government of Britain, for example, would not be giving up its sovereignty to another legislature or to a foreign central bank. *It would be surrendering its power to expropriate its citizens by inflation. Monetary policy would be depoliticised. Neither domestic nor foreign politicians and functionaries would have any control over the money of Europe.*

This suggests that, once the ECOM has been introduced and used for some time, it might well be that an ECOM currency union could be formed for Europe. If the ECOM displaced national currencies to any considerable extent, it would be a natural development to adopt the ECOM as *the* currency for the Community. Indeed, just as the gold standard was widely adopted throughout the world in the 1870s, so might the ECOM, in one or other of its many mutations, be embraced by countries outside Europe — even the United States and Japan. But these are, of course, pipedreams of an inflation-free world.

123

Pros and Cons of the ECOM

When discussing the likely consequences of an ECOM system, one must always specify, as best one can, the best feasible alternative. A point-by-point discussion would try any reader's patience. It might be useful instead to lay out what I believe are the major issues and indicate my judgement about where the balance of advantage lies.

Consider first for Britain the alternative of the free float and a monetary policy that maintains a constant quantity of M0, preferably through the operation of a monetary-base control system. This, I believe, would be superior to the ECOM arrangement. The constancy of the monetary base would ensure that there was no runaway inflation or crushing deflation. True, one would not enjoy the great price stability of the ECOM, but it is often more efficient to adjust to technological progress, changes in the terms of trade (increases in the price of oil, for example), and so on, by allowing exchange rates freedom to move to their market value. The central point is that if markets are not allowed to adjust to exchange rates, then the burden of adjustment will fall on other markets: commodity, labour, money, bond and stock markets. A change in exchange rates is likely to be the best way of making such adjustments.

The objections to this system of monetary-base control with floating exchange rates, compared with the ECOM, are easy to list. The change in the velocity of circulation may be different from the 3 per cent upward trend, a figure commonly found in monetary statistics. (Although I believe it is consistent with the history of the last two or three decades, there is no guarantee that trends can be extrapolated.) The great advantage of the ECOM system is that the velocity adjusts endogenously, whatever happens to the demand for (base) money, to keep the price level constant. There is no opportunity for making mistakes in forecasting money demand; if there are changes in technology or monetary markets that increase the demand for money, then the ECOM system will ensure a response at the fixed price level. There will be no monetary excess or starvation of the economy.

An interesting question is whether it is indeed plausible so to divorce monetary and exchange rate policy from political control. In the case of monetary-base control, I very much doubt it. In practice, in order to deal with liquidity crises and dramatic changes in the public's choice of a cash-deposits ratio, we must allow some overriding discretion to the monetary authorities. This has been demonstrated in many liquidity crises throughout history, and most recently in October 1987. In the ECOM system, however, there is no need for any such override. Provided there is a wide enough spread of reserve assets (and substantial quantities of reserve assets can be sold by making their price attractive), the EIB will provide ample liquidity to prevent any deflationary slump. But would not governments be tempted to 'improve' on the performance of the EIB? Since we lack any relevant experience with such a system, we do not know the answer.[11] If the EIB and the ECOM were the result of a treaty of the EEC governments, however, it would be difficult for a particular government to play fast and loose with its constitutional provisions; but one should not be so sanguine about the institutions of the Community.

Conclusion

In reflecting on monetary constitutions I have wandered a long way from the immediate issues of exchange rates and monetary policy. Yet it is important to inject new ideas into the problems of monetary systems in Europe. I do not believe that the monetary integration of Europe is desirable unless there are considerable obvious gains to be made in this way. The only test of desirability is that people freely choose one currency as the vehicle for their transactions and wealth-holding and accounting. The fabulous success of post-1945 European civilisation was founded on freedom. Liberty is as important in money as in anything else.

NOTES

Chapter 1: Floating and Anchoring Currencies

1. *A Tract on Monetary Reform*, 1923, reprinted in J. M. Keynes, *Collected Writings*, Vol. IV, London: Macmillan for the Royal Economic Society, 1971.

2. The retirement in 1990 of that rock of monetary integrity, Dr Helmut Schlesinger, will provide a good test of the robustness of the institution.

Chapter 2: Ideas on Money and Exchange Rates

1. Unfortunately the word 'flexible' has been taken over by those who eschew free exchange rates and embrace bastardised 'fixed but flexible' exchange rates, such as those in the Exchange Rate Mechanism of the European Monetary System.

2. I wish it were possible to dismiss the thought that exchange controls could conceivably be imposed by some future government of the UK. Alas, it would be folly to ignore the contingency.

3. Of course, aggregate *supply* also plays a crucial role here. I am ignoring supply-side effects only for ease of exposition and certainly not because I believe them to be non-existent or even unimportant.

4. In particular, the idea of consistent or rational expectations takes the position that people will formulate their expectations such that they are consistent with the basic laws of economics which they believe are best applicable to the phenomena they are analysing. In principle, people are maximisers. Those who will survive and prosper will form expectations that are consistent with the 'best' theory. For a first formulation of this idea in macro-economics, see my 'Consistent Expectations, Distributed Lags and the Quantity Theory', *Economic Journal*, Vol. 81, No. 322, June 1971, pp. 273-81. The subject has since become a major preoccupation of many economists, such as Patrick Minford and David Peel, Robert Lucas, and others.

5. It might be worth noting that, if we express the numerator and denominator in dollars, exactly the same result emerges. And the real exchange rate of the United States is the reciprocal.

6. These equalities are the result of goods arbitrage, in the case of steel, and capital arbitrage in the case of money.

7. Strictly speaking, it is not the forward rate that is the predictor of the future spot rate. The true predictor is the *implicit discount* (or premium) — that is, the divergence of the forward rate from its interest-rate parity.

8. Both statements must be qualified since differential real growth may have a significant effect. The monetary expansion is meant to be over and above that required to accommodate the increase in the demand for money accounted for by real growth of GNP. Also there may be systematic shifts in the long-run demand for money. Again these should be accommodated in interpreting the effects of money on exchange rates and inflation.

9. The phenomenon of overshooting is characteristic of many models of the monetary process. I discovered this to be true of Milton Friedman's permanent income demand hypothesis. See my article, 'Professor Friedman on the Demand for Money', *Journal of Political Economy*, Vol. 73, No. 5, October 1965, pp. 545-51.

10. There is another non-monetary reason for the real exchange rate to overshoot in adjusting to a new level. Because the elasticities of supply and demand for goods are normally lower in the short run than in the long run, the real exchange rate will have to move much more in the short run than in the long run. This form of overshooting is inherent whatever the exchange rate régime. See Milton Friedman, 'The Case for Flexible Exchange Rates', in his *Essays in Positive Economics*, Chicago: University of Chicago Press, 1953.

11. This argument implicitly assumes that trade is dominated by manufactures where stickiness is thought to be evident. If trade is dominated by commodities then it is a different story.

12. Such a reverse must take place since it is illogical and quite inconsistent with the evidence to suppose that, by increased monetary injections, one can always raise output growth, albeit temporarily in the 6-18 month period, without growth dropping *below* its trend line afterwards. Any such scenario would enable a country to inflate and increase the long-run level of its GNP. This reversal of the original output boost will, through the reduced demand for money, exert a downward

pressure again on interest rates which may in turn lead to a secondary exchange rate boost.

13. Because of the repetition of this view in his innumerable articles in the *Financial Times*, Mr Samuel Brittan is certainly the best-known advocate of this fixation.

14. This presupposes that the fixed rate overshoots in the same way as the floating rate, namely through the current account. But a modest amount of uncovered arbitrage could offset the current account swing and thus may obviate any large interest rate movements. Strictly, as we show later, such movements should be ruled out because of uncovered arbitrage of all kinds.

15. Governments have many occasions to enter the market in conducting ordinary government business, such as buying imports or providing or receiving aid. Such transactions would not be *intervention* in the sense that their purpose is not to influence the exchange rate.

16. The two definitions of sterilization cover a multitude of other sub-definitions. Obviously with the quantity-of-money-constant definition, there are as many definitions of sterilization as there are concepts of 'money'. It is important also to note that because interest rates and money have no exact or unique one-to-one relationship, there are in practice bound to be *some* monetary effects of sterilized intervention. And the larger the intervention, the more likely that these effects will be large. It will also be clear that intervention with sterilization is likely to affect the term structure of interest rates, which will again have monetary effects. In other words, complete sterilization is elusive and ultimately impossible.

17. M. Mussa, 'The Role of Official Intervention', in Leo Melamed (ed.), *The Merits of Flexible Exchange Rates; an Anthology*, Fairfax, Virginia: George Mason University Press, 1988, p. 331-60.

Chapter 3: Money and Exchange Rates in Practice

1. Experience suggests that readers may have some difficulty in accepting this somewhat startling conclusion, namely, that with *absolutely fixed exchange rates*, the interest rates in all maturities must be the same. If the rate of return was greater in the UK than in the USA, then it would pay anyone with dollars to transfer at the ever-fixed exchange rate into pounds and thus earn the higher interest confident in the fact that he could get back into dollars at any time. Such a massive capital inflow into sterling financial assets would ensure that their rates fell, and US rates rose, until they were again equal. Thus does

capital arbitrage ensure the equality. In practice, however, there was a little flexibility since the exchange rates were fixed within a narrow band such as $2.78 to $2.82. Thus, even under conditions of free capital movements, interest rate differentials were possible and even considerable at the very short end.

2. I reviewed the arguments and evidence of the decreasing efficacy, even perversity, of fiscal policy, and the increasing impact of monetary policy, in *Britains's Economic Renaissance; Margaret Thatcher's Reforms 1979-1984*, Oxford University Press, 1986. The last five years (1984-89) have been consistent with, indeed have reinforced, these findings. The swing from fiscal deficit to large fiscal surplus over these years, particularly in 1987-89, certainly had no visible effect in depressing the economy. On the contrary, the economy boomed along with the substantial increase in the rate of monetary growth. This argument is pursued in Chapter 6.

3. For example, Mr Balladur urged a return to a Bretton Woods type of system using some sort of commodity standard, rather than the dollar, in *The Wall Street Journal*, 23 February 1988. The article reviews also the alleged defects of the floating rate system but, alas, his criticisms collapse when one considers alternatives to the floating rate system. Paraphrasing Churchill, floating rates are an awful system, but the alternatives are far worse.

4. The conventional wisdom is that the inflation of 1972-75 was a consequence of the *breakdown* of Bretton Woods. The real culprit was the monetary expansion that began in the mid-1960s and continued through to 1972 or 1973. (The inflation was initially repressed through prices and wage controls in all the main OECD countries.)

5. It is obvious why the dollar was undervalued in the decade or so after the Second World War. Low inflation due to responsible monetary and fiscal policies together with a domination of free-world production all helped. Sterling was a more dubious case. However, the very large devaluation in 1947 did probably undervalue sterling until the British inflation, relative to those of our trading partners, eroded it by the latter half of the 1950s.

6. See Michael R. Darby and James R. Lothian, 'The International Transmission of Inflation', in Michael Bordo (ed.), *Money, History and International Finance: Essays in Honor of Anna J. Schwartz*, University of Chicago Press, 1989, pp. 203-36.

7. This argument about the appropriate ambient conditions for

pegged exchange rates was put by Mr Lawson in his television interview with Mr Brian Walden in November 1989.

8. See Michael Mussa, 'Nominal Exchange Rate Regimes and the Behaviour of Real Exchange Rates: Evidence and Implications', *Carnegie Rochester Conference Series on Public Policy*, No. 24, 1986, pp. 117-224.

Chapter 4: Monetary Policy and International Co-ordination

1. It will be recalled that, in the short run, one cannot predict which way the exchange rate will move. Ultimately, however, there will be an increase in the dollar value of the mark.

2. 'Co-ordination' has been given a great variety of meanings. At its most innocuous level it involves merely the exchange of information between governments. Such information must be confidential or otherwise there would be no point. (For my part, I cannot see why governments withhold such information from the private sector if it is at all valuable for judging the future of economies.) At the highest level, co-ordination has been used to describe an international or multinational plan with specific roles allocated to the participating states. Most people use some concept between these two extremes.

3. One interesting example is the behaviour of the yen in 1989. Virtually everyone was predicting that, because of the large surplus, the yen would have to appreciate relative to the dollar. Indeed, at a conference in February 1988, Rudiger Dornbusch argued that 'the superior performance of Japan in manufacturing and trade requires real appreciation as the classical response ... a move *away* from PPP is required as an adjustment to these favourable developments for the Japanese economy'. Many distinguished economists also thought that the yen must appreciate. (Incidentally, I also thought it likely that the yen would go up in value.) In 1989, however, the yen's effective exchange rate *fell* by 10 per cent, and against the dollar the fall was even larger.

4. For example, in the 1960s the United States followed an inflationary policy in response to short-term political interests (to finance the Vietnam and poverty wars). It is doubtful if any solemn multilateral undertaking not to use inflationary finance would have had any noticeable effect on the behaviour of the administration. (There is of course another explanation: economic ignorance. The economists who advised on policy believed that there would be no substantial inflation because of the presence of unemployment, at least until the 1968 tax increase.)

5. In fact, the December to December consumer price index rose to 13.3 per cent in 1979.

6. It is necessary to add the usual caveat: we do not know what the path would have been in the absence of Plaza. It is conceivable that the dollar was due to reverse and rise dramatically from October onwards, and that the Plaza agreement saved us from such a continued overvaluation. In view of the expansionary monetary policy from 1985 on, this seems very unlikely, though, I concede, not impossible.

7. The G7 countries are a group of the seven largest industrial nations in the world: the USA, Germany, Japan, France, Italy, UK and Canada.

8. See Ronald I. McKinnon, 'Monetary and Exchange Rate Policies for International Financial Stability: A Proposal', *Journal of Economic Perspectives*, Vol. 2, Winter 1988, pp. 83-103.

9. John Williamson and Marcus Miller, 'Targets and Indicators: A Blueprint for the International Coordination of Economic Policy', *Policy Analyses in International Economics*, No. 22, Washington DC: Institute for International Economics, September 1987. See also Jacob Frenkel and Morris Goldstein, 'A Guide to Target Zones', *IMF Staff Papers*, 33, Washington DC, 1986, and Gottfried Haberler, 'The International Monetary System and Proposals for International Policy Coordination', in Phillip Cagan (ed.), *Deficits, Taxes and Economic Adjustments: Contemporary Economic Problems*, Washington DC: American Enterprise Institute, 1987, pp. 62-98.

10. See Samuel Brittan, 'Reference ranges rule, O.K.?', *Financial Times*, 2 June 1988. Brittan appears to think that 'reference ranges' differ from 'target zones' in having what are called soft edges — that is, there is no commitment to intervene, only an obligation to consult.

11. For a detailed blow-by-blow account of the Plaza to Louvre, see Yoishi Funabashi, *Managing the Dollar: From the Plaza to the Louvre*, Washington DC: Institute for International Economics, 1988.

Chapter 5: Monetary Systems for Europe

1. It is noteworthy that the issue of monetary union is not mentioned either in the Treaty of Rome or in the Single European Act (SEA). It is easy to see why it did not appear in 1957, when currencies were still inconvertible, but it is not so easy to see why it was not accorded a central place in the 1985 SEA. It is at least plausible to suppose that the governments

would have been more reluctant to agree to an SEA that had monetary union as an explicit aim.

2. For this assessment, see Gottfried Haberler, 'The International Monetary System, The European Monetary System (EMS) and a Single European Currency in a "Single European Market"', in 'Geldwertsicherung und Wirtschaftsstabilität', in Norburt Bub, Dieter Duwendag, Rudolf Richter (eds.), *Festschrift für Helmut Schlesinger sum 65. Geburtstag,* Frankfurt: Fritz Knapp Verlag, 1990.

3. See Rainer Masera, *L'unifaczione monetaria europea,* Bologna: il Mulino, 1987, for a detailed account of the institutional changes of the 12-13 September 1987 EC Council of Finance Ministers. The Very Short-Term Financing Facility was also lengthened, and there was an agreement to monitor exchange rates and monetary conditions in each of the EMS countries (including, one presumes, the UK).

4. See Helmut Schlesinger, 'Zur weiteren Entwicklung der wahrungsspolitischen Kooperation auf internationaler und europaischer Ebene', *Deutsche Bundesbank,* Auszuge aus Presscartikeln, No. 84, Frankfurt, 17 November 1988.

5. The institutions of Bretton Woods, however, did not accept the system of equal voting. The votes in the IMF and World Bank were weighted according to the share-holdings of the participating governments.

6. The dominance of the Bundesbank is a common theme of most contemporary accounts of the EMS: see, for example, Jacques Melitz, 'Monetary Discipline and Cooperation in the European Monetary System: A Synthesis', in Francesco Giavazzi, Stephano Miscossi and Marcus Miller (eds.), *The European Monetary System,* London: Cambridge University Press, 1988. This view has been disputed by Michele Fratianni and Jurgen von Hagen in 'German Dominance in the EMS: the empirical evidence', *Open Economies Review,* Vol. 1, No. 1, pp. 67-88 (Dordrecht: Kluwer Academic Publishers), 1990. Primarily from analysing interest-rate policies, they argue that the Bundesbank's policy is largely independent of the policies of its fellow-ERM countries. But that does not mean that the Bundesbank *dominates* the others. France and Italy, through realignments and financial controls, *can* diverge from the Bundesbank line if they so wish.

7. The central banks of France and Italy, like the Bank of England, are simply creatures of the government. In Europe only the central bank of Switzerland has an independence approximating that of the Bundesbank.

8. There is an enormous and rapidly growing literature on this subject. My selected reading would include: Michele Fratianni, 'The European Monetary System: How well has it worked?', in James A. Dorn and William A. Niskanen (eds.), *Dollars, Deficits and Trade*, Washington DC: Cato Institute, 1989; Roland Vaubel, Comments on Manfred Wegner, 'The European Monetary System: A Regional Bretton Woods or an Institutional Innovation', in J. Vosgerau (ed.), *New Institutional Arrangements for the World Economy*, Berlin: Springer-Verlag, 1989; and Patrick Minford, *European Monetary Union and 1992*, Selsdon Group Special Paper, London: Selsdon Group, 1989.

9. The bases for these statements is contained in Horst Ungerer, Owen Evans, Thomas Mayer and Philip Young, *The European Monetary System; Recent Developments*, International Monetary Fund, Occasional Papers 48, Washington DC: IMF, 1986. Note that Ungerer's analysis ceases with 1985, so it covers the period when the major countries were not conducting massive intervention, and in particular Britain was not shadowing the Deutschemark. From 1986 onwards the results have been confounded by many attempts to influence the dollar, yen and Deutschemark in the Plaza, Louvre I and Louvre II accords. Even so, analyses that cover the whole decade do not materially change the general results. See Michele Fratianni and Jurgen von Hagen, 'The European Monetary System Ten Years After', Discussion Paper 419, Indianapolis: Indiana University Graduate School of Business, September 1989.

10. The best summary of all the experience on inflation and growth rates is to be found in Roland Vaubel, *op. cit.*.

11. See Paul de Grauwe, Memorandum in: *Memoranda on the European Monetary System*, of the Treasury and Civil Service Committee, *The Financial and Economic Consequences of UK Membership of the European Communities*, London: House of Commons, 1985.

12. The results are to be found in A. Hughes-Hallet and Patrick Minford, 'The European Monetary System — does it achieve its aims?', Konstanz Seminar on Monetary Theory and Policy, 1989, Liverpool University, Liverpool. The Liverpool model of the world economy has been used extensively to explore many issues of fiscal and monetary policy.

13. See Francesco Giovazzi and Alberto Giovannini, *Limiting Exchange Rate Flexibility: The European Monetary System*, Cambridge, Mass.: MIT Press, 1989.

14. On the effects of the EMS on Bundesbank behaviour during the

Plaza and Louvre accords, see Yoishi Funabashi, *Managing the Dollar: From the Plaza to the Louvre*, Washington DC: Institute for International Economics, 1988.

15. In his post-resignation interview with Mr Brian Walden on television's *Weekend World*, Mr Lawson, when commending 'managed' exchange rates, mentioned the gold standard as an illustration of a managed system. The main point about the gold standard, of course, was that it was *not* managed; it is the prime example of an automatic, self-regulating system.

16. The reductions in the dispersion of inflation rates over the period 1985-89 have resulted in a period of three years, up to January 1990, when there were no realignments.

17. I discussed this process in *Britain's Economic Renaissance* (Oxford, 1986), and, in application to the current situation in Britain, in articles in the *Financial Times*, 6 April 1988, *The Times*, 3 June 1988, and, finally, in the *Independent*, 'Money on a Roller-Coaster', 14 July 1988. At the end of that July, I was asked to keep quiet and cease publishing. I did.

18. Francesco Giavazzi and Luigi Spaventa, 'The "New" EMS', CEPR Paper No. 369, London: Centre for Economic Policy Research, 1990.

19. A typical example of the attitude appeared in an article by Sarah Hogg, then economics editor of *The Independent*, on 15 July 1988, in response to my criticism in the same newspaper of 14 July.

20. 'The EMS Without a Safety Net', *The Economist*, 27 January 1990, p. 71.

21. Daniel Gros and Niels Thygesen, 'The Institutional Approach to Monetary Union in Europe', Draft Paper, Centre for European Studies, Brussels, 4 May 1990. Professor Thygesen was a member of the Delors Committee, while Daniel Gros was Adviser, Directorate-General for Economic and Financial Affairs of the Commission of the European Communities.

22. It is perhaps appropriate, by analogy, to call the Plaza and Louvre agreements 'half-Bakered' solutions.

23. See Guy de Jonquieres, 'The break with French tradition', *Financial Times*, 17 January 1990. He quotes a foreign banker as saying: 'The authorities haven't bitten the bullet by signalling to the local market that it has to compete internationally'. France's high tax on capital income may well encourage a larger outflow over the longer term.

24. It may appear surprising that these covert exchange controls have not played a more important role in Treasury and other

discussions about the EMS. In *Britain's Economic Renaissance, op. cit.*, I talked about the 'restraints on the free flow of capital' but I was not aware of the true state of affairs until 1988. Most commentators ignore them and just remark on the remarkable reduction of exchange controls — with no great effects on the EMS. It is noteworthy that, at the summit meeting in Madrid in June 1989, the Prime Minister, in setting conditions for the time to join the ERM, required that such regulations and controls should be eliminated.

Chapter 6: Exchange Rate Policies and Politics

1. I confess to being most unsure about the advantages claimed for an exchange rate peg as a necessary element of a monetary reform programme. It has failed in Argentina, Brazil and Chile in the 1980s. The seemingly effective case in Israel turns out, on examination, to be quite different from appearances. Israel fixed to the dollar in 1985, but this was just at the peak of the dollar value. From 1985 the dollar fell precipitously, and this ensured that the *effective* exchange rate of the shekel also fell. The nominal fix was not an effective fix. By 1989, however, Israel's rate of inflation had risen again to 20 per cent. Bolivia is also a case where the exchange rate fix appeared to work well — but again it was over the same lucky time-period. The essential element in both, albeit partial, successes was the reduction in the monetary growth rate.

2. See John B. Wood and Robert Miller, *Exchange Controls for Ever?*, Research Monograph 33, London: Institute of Economic Affairs, 1979.

3. For arguments on this point, see my *Britain's Economic Renaissance: Margaret Thatcher's Reforms 1979-1984*, London: Oxford University Press and American Enterprise Institute, 1986, particularly p. 142, and pp. 160 *et seq.*

4. This fall in the nominal exchange rate was even sharper than the fall in 1981.

5. It is worth noting that the Government had taken many precautions against capital flight. First, there had been an extensive issue of indexed gilts which would protect the holders against a Labour (or Conservative) inflation. Secondly, after the election the Government developed 'Maggie Mae's', a conventional gilt with the option of switching into an indexed instrument. In the event, the capital flight was minimal.

6. As we shall show, the interest rate would have had to have risen

to at least 17 per cent and probably 20 per cent to hold that central value of DM4.3.

7. I believe I first met Mr Lawson shortly after my attack on Mr Heath's policies in 1972. Then I had always thought him a kindred spirit. After the fall of the Heath government, Mr Lawson was an important discussant in developing a new economic policy.

8. In a memorandum dated 6 December 1985, I wrote: 'If monetary growth (M0) is held at its present level (i.e., virtually zero) for a period of two or three years, then it is likely that inflation will fall to about zero before the end of the 1980s and perhaps even by 1988. At last we shall have price stability.' I had left my government employment in 1984, but, as an interested citizen, I still offered my views.

9. The annual rate of growth of sterling M3 had increased from 8.2 per cent in September 1984 to 10.0 per cent by February 1985. By the end of the year, however, the growth rate had risen to nearly 14 per cent. The Chancellor was, in my view rightly, convinced that sterling M3 was a misleading indicator of monetary stringency. One should not ignore it, but in view of the rapid changes in credit markets, it was very difficult to interpret.

10. Note that the reduction in the exchange rate of the Deutschemark was only from DM3.9 to 3.6 — about 8 per cent — during the year ending February 1985. By July 1985 the rate had risen to about DM4.0.

11. For example, Phillips & Drew, 'The Death of Monetarism', *Market Review*, May 1985, and de Zoete & Bevan, *Weekly Economic Survey*, Issue 85/19, 16 May 1985. The 'death' of monetarism has, of course, been pronounced many times. In my recollection, the earliest declaration was by John Kenneth Galbraith in 1980. The City commentators, however, presented serious argument to support their case. The most sophisticated analysis of the situation was given by Gordon Pepper in Greenwell's *Monetary Bulletin*, No. 172, May 1985. He argued that the growth of M3 was primarily due to the increase in real interest rates, and was not a harbinger of inflation. But he did strongly, and in my view rightly, condemn the inefficiency of the demand-side control of monetary aggregates.

12. In his Mansion House speech in October 1985, the Chancellor had announced that the sterling M3 target had been suspended, and that 'The inflation rate is judge and jury'.

13. For a number of repetitions of these arguments, see Samuel Brittan's articles which began with his conversion in the *Financial*

Times, 14 November 1985, with 'Now, alas, it is time to join the EMS' (he meant the ERM).

14. See Charles Goodhart, 'The Conduct of Monetary Policy', *Economic Journal,* Vol. 99, No. 396, June 1989, p. 293. The rule refers not to the Deutschemark but to the effective exchange rate index. The fall in the effective exchange rate over this period was of the order of 20 per cent. But the defence of the central parity in the ERM is effectively with respect to the mark, so in these very rough calculations I have assumed the same rule applies to the mark-sterling rate as to the effective rate.

15. This is a moot point since the '4 to 1' calculation was over the period which included the`shadowing' of the Deutschemark.

16. The G5 are the USA, Japan, UK, Germany and France.

17. William Keegan in *Mr Lawson's Gamble,* London: Hodder and Stoughton, 1989, reported that senior officials in the Treasury were entirely surprised by the Chancellor's announcement at the IMF in 1987 that exchange rates were the main guide for monetary (interest rate) policy. The decision to 'shadow' the Deutschemark had not been considered in depth or detail by officials. It was represented as the consequence of a number of discussions between Mr Lawson and Sir Terence Burns, with offstage assistance from that most distinguished of financial journalists, Mr Samuel Brittan.

18. See 'Company Profitability and Finance', in *Bank of England Quarterly Bulletin,* Vol. 29, No. 1, August 1989, p. 377.

19. The supply-side changes have been analysed in detail by Patrick Minford, 'Europe and the Supply Side', in Gerhard Fels and George M. von Fuerstenberg (eds.), *A Supply-side Agenda for Germany,* Berlin: Springer-Verlag, 1989, pp. 47-71.

20. Gordon Pepper shows that the net effect on M4 of foreign exchange reserves in 1987 was £7.2 billion. He concludes, however, that although the authorities failed to 'sterilize' (in the sense of having no direct effects on M4) all the intervention in 1987, they did manage to catch up in the first quarter of 1988. (G. T. Pepper, *Money, Credit and Inflation,* Research Monograph 44, London: Institute of Economic Affairs, 1990, p. 48.)

21. More important internationally was the reduction in the yen discount rate to 2.5 per cent in order to prop up the dollar. This contributed to a massive real estate and stock market inflation in 1989-90.

22. Most of the other major OECD countries appear to have acted with a prudence similar to that of the United States. Britain was the odd man out, followed by Japan.

23. There is still room for debate about whether the monetary squeeze from 1988 onwards was too tight or still too loose. There was no doubt at all that interest rates of at least 12 per cent were required in order to get the growth of the monetary base under some sort of control.

24. In his speech at the Party Conference in October 1989, only days after the increase of base rates from 14 to 15 per cent, the Chancellor made it clear that the Conservative party would not be 'the party of devaluation'.

25. Reports appeared in the media that I was opposed to the increase in interest rates to 15 per cent in October 1989. Other reports said I supported the increase. My position was that we were in no position to change the market expectations, and that moving up to 15 per cent was the least bad alternative.

26. See *Bank of England Quarterly Bulletin*, Table 17.1. Note that I am including only convertible currencies and excluding gold, and the IMF reserve and SDRs.

27. In 1984 I ignored the $2.5 billion floating rate note issue which the Treasury issued for the specific purpose of increasing the reserves. Clearly this issue had potential ERM entry in mind.

28. *Bank of England Quarterly Bulletin*, Vol. 29, No. 3, August 1989, p. 377. A more conservative calculation may take the point that a 12 per cent rate of return cannot be sustained and that a 10 per cent, or even an 8 per cent, rate would be more appropriate in the long run.

29. See 'External Balance Sheet of the United Kingdom', in *Bank of England Quarterly Bulletin*, Vol. 28, No. 4, pp. 520-27. The net asset position grew from £12.1 billion at the end of 1979 to £113.2 billion and £89.5 billion at the end of 1986 and 1987 respectively. Such assets are obviously in part acquired by the cumulation of current balance surpluses, but this can only account for some £17 billion in the published statistics. (The reader may well believe that the current account balance is much underestimated in the official statistics. But even if we double it to £34 billion, it still cannot account for the bulk of the additional net foreign assets.) The balance is largely accounted for by the yield, and in particular the capital gain including currency revaluation, on such foreign assets. On certain assets the Bank has calculated the full rate of return on assets (not net assets) — see chart 6, p. 525. This suggests that the full rate of return has been about 20 per cent over the period from the end of 1979 to the end of 1986. This appears to be the nominal rate

of return, so the real rate of return would be somewhat lower, but almost certainly in excess of 15 per cent.

30. Historically, the fee or royalty charged by the monarch for the unfettered right to mint coins from bullion — now the state's sole right to control the mainly paper currency of a country.

Chapter 7: A Monetary Constitution for Europe

1. Deflation, it will be noted, increases the attraction of money as a store of value and increases, if anything, its use as an intermediator. As a standard of account, it may suffer somewhat, but not if the deflation is gentle (as in the United States after the Civil War).

2. A. Meltzer, 'Some Evidence on the Comparative Uncertainty Experienced under Different Monetary Regimes', in Colin D. Campbell and William R. Dougan (eds.), *Alternative Monetary Regimes*, Baltimore: Johns Hopkins University Press, 1986.

3. The United States went on a bimetallic standard in 1792, but as the price of gold rose relative to that of silver, so silver drove out gold; America was then on a *de facto* silver standard for some 40 years.

4. See Michael Bordo, 'Bimetallism', in John Eatwell, Murray Milgate and Peter Newman (eds.), *The New Palgrave Dictionary of Economics*, London: Macmillan, 1987.

5. See Albert Gailord Hart, 'Commodity Reserve Currency', in Eatwell, Milgate, and Newman (eds.), *The New Palgrave Dictionary of Economics, ibid*. Lord Kaldor was the primary force behind these suggestions.

6. See Irving Fisher, *The Purchasing Power of Money*, New York: Macmillan, 2nd edition, 1913. Warren L. Coats has developed these ideas in 'In Search of a Monetary Anchor: A New Monetary Standard', *IMF Working Paper*, Washington DC: IMF, 11 October 1989.

7. The seminal paper is Robert L. Greenfield and Leland B. Yeager, 'A Laissez-Faire Approach to Monetary Stability', *Journal of Money, Credit and Banking*, Vol. 15, August 1983, pp. 302-15. See also Irving Fisher, *Stabilizing the Dollar*, New York: Macmillan, 1920.

8. For a clear account of the process of arbitrage, see Warren Coats (1989), *op. cit.*

9. It might be thought that the yield on the TB would move to abort such arbitrage. True, it may move slightly, but the yield will be constrained by the substitutability into parallel in-

struments — even ordinary treasury bills or perhaps indexed treasuries which do not have the status of reserve assets.

10. J. Riboud, *The Case for a New ECU: Towards Another Monetary System*, London: Macmillan, 1989.

11. One form of 'improvement' might be to specify the currency in terms of a *constant rate of inflation*, say, 3 per cent per annum. This could be done easily in the ECOM framework, and it might be argued that, because of downward rigidities in the prices, such a constant inflation would involve reduced frictional costs. In my view, however, adding 3 per cent to all prices and wages will not solve problems of rigidities.